To Ivin
wishing you
a happy 60th
Birthday

OUR SECRET MOVIE

Lots of
Love
from
Sonya. X

Sonya Knezovich

authorHOUSE®

AuthorHouse™ UK Ltd.
500 Avebury Boulevard
Central Milton Keynes, MK9 2BE
www.authorhouse.co.uk
Phone: 08001974150

First published by AuthorHouse   3/24/2011

ISBN: 978-1-4389-2742-8 (sc)
ISBN: 978-1-4389-2741-1 (hc)

Acknowledgements

First of all I would like to thank my wonderful husband, Ivan, and our two great children, my son Kash and my daughter Karrie, for their unselfish support and for allowing me time to write this book, but most of all for being in my life.

I would also like to thank all the authors of the books that dare to 'go there'. For it is these people who made me feel I was not alone in my way of thinking, and their books lifted my spirit and encouraged me to write my book. There are far too many to name but I enjoyed them all.

Thank you.

To my own group of special friends. Each and every one of us is special in our own unique way. To honour and be who we truly are is what we are here for.

Sally is organised and we all need that.

Lisa is a talented lady who takes it as far as anyone can.

Kate is at last able to nurture the way she has always wanted to.

Max can now share her vibrancy with as many people as possible.

Fi always manages to make us feel that we are right.

Sue is about to show the world that she is made of love.

Karen has helped us all to be who we are by suffering at her own expense.

Yvette dared to go where we would all like to.

Catharine stood tall against all odds.

Beryl will grow from necessity, which encourages us all.

Barbara is here to mother us all and grace us with her love.

Julie will teach us all how to connect to the planet so we can bring it into our lives.

Shaz has realised that the only problem she has is that she does not have one.

Emme's path is in front of her, as it always has been; only now she can see it.

I would like to mention and thank Eamon Downey for helping me to feel normal, and helping me to see what I am here to do and to be.

A big thank you to John Mc Fadden and Lisa Kabnick for the help and support with the first edit of this book in Italy.

Also a big thank you to Liz for the great days going through the book trying to make it comprehensible.

I am truly grateful for all the people who, like me, are aware that there is far more to existence than what we experience with our five senses, and dare to go there against the odds. Those who dare are the people who truly live.

Contents

Introduction

This book is about my journey to discover the person I was becoming. It is written in a simple way to try to explain the experience we are living. It had never been my intention or desire to put pen to paper, let alone to write a book. But one night's unbelievably strange experience changed everything I thought life and myself to be.

The book begins with a light-hearted fantasy about a time before we were on planet Earth. I show how we can, if we want, play a role in a movie on Earth and talk about how great the story could be. I then move on to the first experiences that happened to me, written as a brief memoir. I try to show the reader the way I now know life to be. The book moves on to discuss how people can discover what I discovered and experience this for themselves, not omitting the resulting effects on them and everything else around them.

I then describe many of the different people and life situations that I have experienced until I reach the point of existence, as I have discovered it to be; my purpose for being here and playing my role in the movie we call life.

The book is designed to help people discover their truth, not mine. But it is through my own process of discovery that they are given the opportunity to wake up to their truth. It has a sense of freedom and common sense that I think we all find acceptable.

It is a natural unfolding of my experiences, and those of the people I teach. It was not designed or structured prior to writing. I had no idea where it was going or what I had to say, only that I felt a burning desire to put words onto paper. It could be termed automatic writing. It was only later that I discovered that the information was coming from a bigger, much bigger part of myself than I was previously aware of.

Neither is this book about teaching rituals or dogma. If anything it is teaching freedom, from the self we believe we are, and from our experiences in life and the information and guidance we have received. It is about taking a fresh look at what and who we think we are and deciding what we want and are capable of being. It is also a reference guide to help people who, instead of learning and growing, get caught in their personal dramas. As people grow and learn they naturally move to another layer of their truth, believing that they know all the answers. However, each new level of awareness has its own set of values. The subjects may be the same but the lessons are not. I try to make the reader aware of this fact. The strange thing about writing this book is that it was as much about my own learning and growing as about helping others to learn and grow. I was both the student and my own teacher.

Since writing this book I have become a very different person. I have grown on both a conscious and a physical level. My awareness and understanding of human nature has also been refined. Even though everything appears slightly different now, I wanted to show how I experienced life at that time, so when people are at that stage of their journey they will be able to connect with that part of the process.

Now I am very busy typing Book Two. How many more books will follow, I don't know, only time will tell. But I continue to grow and learn, so I hope I will have something to teach for as long as I am living. I know that through my writing I can help people to discover their truth.

My name is Sonya Knezovich, I am forty-four years young, five foot five, of average build and with light brown highlighted hair. I am told I am physically attractive and have the ability of attracting people to me, almost in a magnetic way. I am married to an amazing man and we have been together for twenty-five years. I am a mother of two beautiful children: our son, who is now seventeen, and our daughter, who has just turned fifteen. Three really great beings whom I immensely enjoy being and living with. Our only pet is a one-year-old bull mastiff bitch whose name is Nu Nu. We live in a secluded country home on the edge of a large forest in Worcestershire. I have two sisters, and we are extremely close to my mother, who is more like an older sister to us. We love her dearly. She is married to my stepfather, who I regard as my father. I have many close friends, quite a few of whom live in different countries. Wherever I travel in the world now, I seem to develop new friends through my openness, help and support. I was a normal healthy child with a pretty happy childhood, despite my parents divorcing. I was an average student at school but I struggled with the system. I always felt that I had a wealth of answers but I didn't actually know what were the questions for these answers. I knew I was really intelligent but not in the normal IQ sense. Years later I had a group of my friends over for a psychic evening. Three psychic people with different abilities hosted the evening. Most of the people who came were the normal sceptics, but I always thought that there was more to life than meets the eye. As a gift for having the party at my house I had a free astrological horoscope printed. The astrologist explained the chart, which was full of symbols. When she reached the part relating to intelligence, she said that there was nothing in this section, and a few of my friends started to laugh. She then explained that the reason for this was that our intelligence is way beyond the measurement of IQ; it is of a higher form. She said to me that I was here to do something really big.

The funny thing was that when she said this it made sense to me; it was what I had always known. I do not mean that I am more intelligent than other people, only that what I knew, and could not find an outlet for as yet, seemed to be on this psychic level of awareness, a different level of intelligence and I knew that this was my real vocation.

I rarely thought about that night again as I take everything with a pinch of salt. However, looking back I now completely understand what she said to me. It was probably the beginning of what this book and my life are now about. I am here to activate this higher level of awareness in other people. Because I know mine, which I discovered through many different experiences, I am able to assist other people to find their own. Many different people who I have helped in the past told me that I was psychic. To me, their solutions seemed like common sense; to them it was an uncanny grasp of reality way beyond their imagination.

Clairvoyants that I visited during this time told me much the same thing. 'What are you doing here?' they'd say, or 'You know. You don't need me to tell you'. Some of them wanted to teach me how to use my ability.

Many years earlier there was one man whom I went to see, a spiritualist minister. He told me that by the time I was thirty-six I would have everything that I had ever wanted. I was twenty-eight when I saw this man. He told me lots of other things that have come true, and at thirty-six I did have everything that I had ever wanted. I was married to the man I loved, I had two healthy children, a nice house in the country, my own business and a full and happy life. At this time the Lottery had just started, and I thought that maybe he meant that I would win. Of course I didn't.

Beyond reaching this point in life he never told me what would happen the day I turned thirty-seven. My life changed drastically. I know now that I did win the Lottery. Not the money lottery, the life lottery. I found the secret to happiness; I found me.

At this time I had trained in nail and beauty treatments and eventually started a business in the beauty field in my local town. The salon itself was in a very old and haunted building which was full of history. After a few years of enjoyable work with my local lady customers I closed my business down. I realised by then that I was far too generous to be a good businesswoman. The rest is still unfolding but I now run workshops and help people discover themselves by going beyond what they think they are. I also help them with their problems, much like an agony aunt. To further enhance my skills, I completed a course in social counselling, but it was not what I needed to do.

The way I work with people is normally on a one-to-one basis, so there is only so much time I have to help. Writing a book enables me to reach many more people.

Besides all of this I travel frequently with my husband on his overseas trips. Most years I visit South Africa and the USA, but wherever I go I always work on people. It just happens on planes, at parties or on a beach. It is as if I have a flashing beacon on my head that attracts people to me. And they all tell me their different reasons for speaking to me or wanting to speak to me. I once had a lady follow me around at a seminar. She told me she was sorry for following me, but my voice made her feel the same way as when she was playing her Indian meditating drum.

I live a very comfortable life and most of the time it is pure pleasure. I think that this radiates out from me. There is a side to me that is shy, although no one who knows me would believe that. I have a giving and sharing nature, though I don't like people to expect things from me. I still have the same life situation and problems as everyone else; I just understand them, and most of the time let them go, let them be. This makes life an experience, not a problem.

Preface

First, there was,
Which was nothing in truth.
Second, there was awareness.
From awareness came I.
Awareness created I.
So I thought.
I created to discover I.
Creation gave I the ability to know I created all, was all and nothing before awareness and creation, which came first.
Everything else is of this.
I in creation and all creation is the truth and non-truth.
Third is the ability to discover that truth, within a reality.
The book before you is all about the passage above. It is my discovery of the secret that is hidden within all of our lives.

Chapter 1

This is a book about our lives; yes, yours as well as mine. It is a book about the movie we are now living.

I want you to imagine that you are not sitting here on Earth reading this book, but that you are in some other place that has a different set of natural laws and a different reality. Imagine that a long time ago you had a thought, which created the person you are now and the role that you are playing. That thought started a process that you are now living. You're playing a role in the movie that came from that thought. You are the main character in the movie as well as the creator who thought it into existence. So not only are you the creator/author, director and actor, you also get the opportunity to be the critic.

Bear with me and I will explain. You become the critic by discovering your truth. When we are playing our part in our movie we have our memory of who we truly are removed. When we play our part in the movie we play it for real. We believe it is real. The purpose of our life here on Earth lies in the discovery of our true self; it is in the unravelling of our secret.

In his role on Earth our protagonist gets a human body that has five senses, which enables him to feel that everything is real, and he feels separate from others because his body has this thick skin all around it. On Earth, we get to experience all those things that we are not able to in our truth.

Our character on Earth is permanently changing and evolving. During our life we will all reach a point when we have the opportunity to open up to our truth, when we will discover that we are in fact just one part of the truth. We will instinctively discover our true nature, with the assistance of our sixth sense, which is the connection between the body and our truth, a sort of intercom. This is where the fun begins.

I want to tell you about life and beyond the way I have discovered it to be, but in order for me to do that through these words, you need to pay attention to them.

We are all individual and respond in our own unique way, but just for one moment I am appealing to the common threads that we all have. Please give yourself time and space to read these words and look deeply into what they are saying. In their simplicity there is a secret that can change your life for the better. These words can achieve this only if you find freedom from what you think you know. Freedom only sits in a moment of now, so try and stop time, judgment and need. Free yourself to discover your secret.

This book has been written in two parts. The first is the 'how to', the second is how I discovered the 'how to'. They are, however, entwined throughout, so prepare to be a little confused but do try to follow.

This is the way I choose to tell you what I know and I have always known. I didn't realise that I did know. I had not yet reached the point in my journey when I was able to know. Now that I do, I realise that I'm here on the planet using this book about my movie to help you remember, just like me. For some people reading this book, this story of my life, is all they need to remind them who they really are, because this book and these words are part of their movie. A wake-up call is what this book is all about. We simply just start to remember things as our secret unfolds.

What actually get us to that point in our movie? This varies from person to person. It depends on what is written in your movie and also whether my book is part of your movie. I guess that because you're reading this, it must be. If you find these thoughts strange, the rest is going to really confuse you, but hang in there if you can.

This book is just unfolding. There is no plan or structure. I am writing it in what I call free flow. Words, thoughts or experiences just happen, and then I write. Although, in my truth, this is laid down in my contract. It was always by design.

At this point I would like to brief you on my movie. It would be a good idea if you jotted down some details of your movie (your life) to review.

Chapter 2
My Movie

Sunday, 30 November 1958. This is the day that I was born, the second daughter of John and Barbara. We were living in Germany as my father was in the British Army. I don't remember much about Germany. We moved from Germany to Yorkshire in England when I was a child and my first memories seem to start there. Just everyday events like riding my new tricycle and meeting local friends. I was three years old.

We then moved to Kidderminster, we being my mother, father and my older (by twenty months) sister Karen and myself. I was four or five years old and we stayed with our grandparents for a while. My parents bought and moved into a new house, a very modern split-level design. We lived there until my parents got divorced when I was about fifteen.

I was a happy, easygoing little girl even when my parents divorced. I stayed with my mother and my sister after the divorce, and Karen got married around about the same time. After I finished school I went into various jobs, not feeling especially passionate about any particular career. I trained as a hairdresser and studied beauty therapy at college on day-release. Then I moved on. I was a manager of a clothing shop, worked in catering for quite a while and qualified as a catering manager.

At the age of nineteen, I met and fell in love with a great man, who I still love with all my heart. We now have two children, Kash and Karrie. Both are really great kids. I have condensed my life because it would fill another book. There have been many wonderful, mind-blowing events and also many sad times – all in all a well-balanced, average family life. Eventually I settled back into the beauty field and opened up a nail bar and beauty salon in our local town.

November 30 1995. My thirty-seventh birthday.

Ivan, my husband, had gone to South Africa on business. This time he took my younger sister (by seventeen years, from my mother's second marriage) with him. I talked her into going to experience a different way of life. She is back now after living and working there for five years. She now lives in Scotland with her South African husband, whom she met and fell in love with while she was there. I was in the process of opening another section of my business. Ladies' accessories (handbags, belts, etc.) seemed to fit in with the nail bar and beauty rooms that we already had. In the middle of it, I left to make an appointment at the hairdresser's for a colour and cut, my birthday treat. My hair appointment was with Lisa, a good friend who was also a customer of ours. Lisa did a really great job colouring my hair, but it was another girl in the salon who cut my hair and I think she got a bit carried away. On the way home I felt incredibly upset, which was unusual for me. I'd never had hang-ups about my hair in the past. No matter how drastic it might be, my motto was always 'well, it will soon grow'. But this time I felt so angry I could have driven the car into a wall. This anger was powerful. It seemed to come from nowhere. It was as if all the anger I'd ever felt, buried deep inside me, had surfaced like a giant boil.

When I arrived back at the shop, all the girls liked my hair and they didn't understand why I was so angry. Nor did I. We carried on, had a good evening pricing goods and doing all the displays. By midnight the shop was looking great, ready for the grand opening the following morning.

The next day went well. We had a good response from the customers and everyone was surprised at how reasonable our prices were. I asked Karen and Max, another good girlfriend, to come over for the evening to celebrate. We decided to have egg and chips (our favourite) for dinner, washed down with a bottle of wine. Tanya, my children's au pair, put Kash and Karrie to bed and Max, Karen and I sat in the conservatory drinking. We chatted about lots of different things before it came up that that a lady who worked as a healer had been in the shop that day for a facial. She told me that I had healing hands. 'Max, come here. See if you can feel anything,' I said with a smile. Max put her arm out, and I ran my hand over it. All of a sudden something incredible happened. She leapt backwards, yelled out and then started crying. 'Max, are you okay? Don't cry, don't cry,' I said, and ran over to her. Max said it felt like a bolt of electricity had shot through her body. I turned to Karen and said, 'Karen, come here and see if it happens to you.' The same sort of thing happened to Karen. Then all kinds of things started happening. The three of us did not know what was going on. There seemed to be some sort of energy in the room and we all started picking up information. It felt like a beam of light or a force coming to me. It was so strong that it felt as if it was coming from a place way beyond our universe. I could sense things; shapes, triangles and squares. I received a message but where it came from I had no idea. It seemed to just burst into my mind. This message was so strong and to the point; it was LET GO. It kept repeating over and over: 'Let go, let go'. I thought at the time that the message was for Karen. We all started experiencing what I can only describe as a surge of energy. It made our bodies quiver and our eyes water. It sounded and looked as if we were crying our eyes out, but without the emotion. It was all very tense, exciting and terrifying. There seemed to be a connection amongst all of us, as if we were all sisters, triplets, sharing the same sensation, almost as if we were one split into three. We were telling each other of the connection we were feeling to other people and even places; it felt like an appointment with destiny. The strangest thing of all was that it felt as if it had happened before, or that I had dreamed this day. The familiarity was so uncanny, and similar things to this continued to happen all night. At six o'clock in the morning we decided to go to bed. We were so scared that we all got into my bed and slept together, holding hands.

The next day at work I started to tell Kate, my partner in the salon, all about what had happened the night before. Whilst I was telling her I had the same feeling as the night before, and Kate was picking it up too. Our eyes were streaming, we were experiencing surges of energy running through our bodies and we both felt the presence of her father, who had died a few years earlier. We had the feeling that he had sent Kate to all of us.

Throughout that week, all kinds of things started happening. I was picking up all sorts of information about different people, time frames and life situations. Every customer I did a treatment on started to tell me about their dead relatives, and most of them would start crying. It became quite a strain. Things were happening to me at home too. I hardly slept because I was afraid to go to sleep, I was afraid of being alone, I was in a constant state of stress that was exciting and terrifying all wrapped up together. I was not eating either.

The main experiences seemed to happen to Max, Karen and myself, although things were also happening to Julie (a good friend), and of course Kate.

Dills, a customer, popped into the shop and dropped off a nice little note thanking me for taking time out to find her a sarong for her holiday. This really touched me and I got really upset. That was it, I ran upstairs and broke down, crying uncontrollably, filled with utter confusion. Karen came upstairs and asked me what was wrong. Then she panicked and ran off to get mom, who, incidentally, knew nothing of the past week's happenings. When mom arrived at the shop she found her daughter staring into the mirror, proclaiming that she could see not one but three faces; one old face, a young female and one male. 'Come away! Come away!' mom urged, but it was too powerful and captivating and really scary at the same time. I was totally transfixed. Karen stepped in and put her arms around me, trying not only to comfort me but also trying to pull me away. Meanwhile Ivan rang. I really could not talk to him at that moment. He phoned another three times, which was not a normal thing for him to do. He must have sensed that something was wrong.

While Karen and I were talking to mom she told me that when I was born there was a skin-like membrane that covered my face. She said that according to an old wives' tale, it meant that I would be blessed with second sight. It was also apparently very lucky. I asked her why she had never told me about it before and she couldn't tell me. She didn't even know why she was telling me now. The night eventually seemed to calm down and we all went home.

My life and the person I knew myself as sure did change from then on. We three saw a number of clairvoyants and they all seemed to pick up on the ability I apparently had. These were the only people we could go to who might understand what was going on with us; if we had gone to see a doctor they might have thought we were mad and referred us to a psychiatrist. We knew that this was happening and we knew it was something different, but most of all we knew we were not mad. One of the mediums I saw was Eamon, who was a friend that I went to school with. I had asked Eamon to come to the shop about six months before all of this had started, the reason being that when I had taken over the second floor of the building; there had been lot of strange things happening. One instance was the sound of a baby crying however we could not find an explanation for any of it. The shop is part of a very old building and was said to be haunted. Eamon explained it as residual energy, just like when we leave a fingerprint. Because I am what is called a 'sensitive', I was able to pick it up. He also told me that the energy I was connecting to was from somewhere way beyond what he was used to picking up.

Ivan came back from South Africa and in between the tears I told him what had been happening. He told me that when he was sixteen he had a strange thing happen to him, which turned him upside down and inside out. Since that day he had felt that he would do the right thing. I seemed to remember him telling me something about it, but I did not think that the experience he'd had was what I went through. Ivan warned me not to meddle too deeply in these things or I might get burned. He suggested that I forget all about it. This was easier said than done.

Chapter 3

So many amazing things have happened to me since my thirty-seventh birthday, but most of them were to my benefit, helping me get to where I am now. From that time, every day in some way, I have been remembering who I am. I now understand the first set of experiences I went through, what they were and why they happened, but it took five years of my journey to understand. I opened myself up to something more than what we normally perceive. I pick up vibrations around and through people and sense what they are feeling. I didn't know that I had chosen that opening, but somehow deep within me I remember that I chose it a long time ago, before I came to Earth (the secret was unfolding). So I have spent the last five years looking, feeling, being and helping other people to do the same. The more I became aware of who I was, the more I became aware of who the other people around me were.

As human beings we have been given minds with which to communicate, to create and to solve. We are given bodies to put our thoughts into action and to interact with one another. We have also been given six senses. We all know what the five senses are because we use them every moment of our lives if we are lucky. But our sixth sense is only ever used in fleeting moments and mainly by women. It is my sixth sense that gives me the connection to be able to write this book. The sixth sense has an immense ability that is very different from all our other senses because it is the part of us that is connected to our true self. The sixth sense gives us access to the part that wrote the book about the movie we are now living.

All of our senses need to be used to their full ability and acknowledged. When we use them the way they were designed to be used, a whole new world starts to open up to us, just as it did when we were children. When we use our sense of touch we must pay attention to what happens to us as our fingers sense that perceived information, which is then converted by our brain into knowledge, then stored in our memory for future reference. We normally need to experience this a number of times before our recall is easily activated.

So life is made up of perceived information and genetic information. Then there is other information that was in no way learned or passed down through the genetic pool. This information is so odd that most of the time we choose to ignore it. When we touch something hot we know it will burn. This is because we have learnt this information and stored it in our memory as youngsters. When we come across something new, we investigate it with our five senses and categorise it.

On that December night in 1995, I became aware of something I did not know or remember feeling before. I tried as hard as I could to find a reasonable explanation for what happened, any explanation. All of my five senses were in overdrive trying to slot it all into a box. I was not seeing it, smelling it, hearing it, tasting it or touching it. I was sensing it. This was having an effect on all of my senses physiologically and psychologically. In other words my mind was trying to understand something I did not know. My eyes were streaming but not with normal emotion. And the hair all over my body was erect and so alive. There was something deep within me that knew this to be real and even familiar, and yet I knew that I had never felt like this before. I was just relieved that the two other people there with me were both experiencing the sensations too. Sanity in unity.

Events come and go. Some events have more impact than others, but all contribute to the whole. Sometimes it is the tiny things that can have the most impact on our lives, if we take the time to pay attention to them and not get lost in them. This way we are able to understand more about what is going on, which, in turn, will allow us to see how all is one. We all contribute to the whole. We all have a part to play, we just need an opportunity to discover and deliver what we know.

This is my 'something' to say. So I begin to tell the story of a love that never ends, a true love, a real love. Your own.

Love is the food of life. To come to know yourself is one of the greatest things you'll ever do and you will continue to benefit from it every second of every day. As I do.

To know your own love is no threat to anyone or anything. It is a gift to all. Don't let your love die or hide it from yourself or others. Embrace it and become it. You will be amazed at how powerful love is. It is a wonderful thing to get to know yourself. It might seem like hard work in the beginning, but I assure you that it gets easier as you go along.

There are many roads that you can take to find yourself. This first road that you have taken is the most important because you decide that there is something missing from your life. You are not sure what it is, but you are willing to look. This thing that you are looking for is not missing, it is just hiding behind a lot of life's experiences and effects, and this thing is YOU.

So to find you, we have to begin to unravel all of those effects.

Chapter 4
Coincidence

One of the very first things that I noticed were the bizarre coincidences happening around me. Everywhere, anywhere, in any situation, coincidences just kept on occurring. So I started to pay more attention to my life. It was as though life was trying to talk to me, tell me something; I just had to figure out what it was.

After a while I decided that there was no such thing as coincidence. Life had a plan. Once I reached this decision my body responded with a really big surge of energy. It was exhilarating and powerful. It truly stopped me in my tracks.

It took me quite a while to discover that when I made a decision about life, and it was right, I would experience a surge of energy. This surge was confirmation. After I realised this, it was a matter of saying things and breaking my thoughts down until I got my confirmation. I worried that maybe I was able to make these surges happen, so I'd try my best to bring them on. Nothing I did could make it happen. So I finally accepted it as a 'yes' to my questioning. I would have pictures of a scene appear in my mind. The picture obviously meant something but I had no idea what. I decided to say what the scene made me feel and then I felt a surge. On other occasions, I would see an image and say what I was feeling and I would not experience a surge, so then I would say out loud what the scene was showing me and, hey presto! the surge would come. What I started to realise was that I was learning a new way of communicating. It was very different to what we know in our everyday lives, but I soon got the hang of it. What I did not know was who or what I was communicating with. It was a few years before I really understood what was going on and why.

Discovering coincidences felt to me as if life was presenting me with a picture. This picture was so way off the wall that I couldn't fail to pay attention to it. The great thing was that by paying attention to it, more events seemed to happen. You could call these things that happened silly, ridiculous even, but whatever we call them they were happening.

I was in my shop one day, thinking to myself how it would be really nice to learn the history of this place and find out why it was haunted. All of the girls in the shop said they would like to know too. Two weeks later I was in the staffroom when Karen came running in and said, 'You are not going to believe this, come out here and meet this woman.' This lady had come into the shop and her daughter was booking her an appointment for a massage. She had told Karen that her grandmother had owned the building and that she had lived there when she was a little girl with many other people. The building was a shop and her grandmother's home, which she divided up into tenements. We got talking and she told us so many different things that gave us answers to our questions about the place. It was a merchant's house many years before her grandmother had owned it. One of the events that she told us about was that of the crying baby we had all heard. The baby's mother had fallen down the stairs while pregnant and the fall had brought on the birth of the baby, who only lived about three weeks, but from the moment it was born it never stopped crying. We were all very taken aback by this, as we had heard this crying for a long time. But after that day we never heard the crying baby again. The lady told us that her grandmother had a shop just like the one I had just opened downstairs and said she would bring a picture in to show us. It was quite interesting that all these years later I had opened up the same type of shop, considering that I had started with a nail bar, then incorporated a beauty salon, and that the shop was never something that I wanted to do, it just sort of popped into my mind one day out of the blue. A couple of weeks later the lady returned to the shop with the picture, which was quite uncanny. She also brought in the death certificate of the baby, which had been kept with the pictures. The date she came back to the shop was 12 April. We read the death certificate and saw that the baby had died in this building sixty years earlier to the day. Of course, I started surging with energy and felt a great sense of relief. It was as if I had solved a puzzle.

One of the other things she told us was that there was a lady of the night who had lived in one of the tenements and had drowned in the river. Her name was Rose. When she said this I had such an overwhelming feeling because a month earlier we had a lady who was clairvoyant in the building, and she was trying to get me to use my ability, which she knew I had. She wanted me to say what I was picking up, and one of the things that I kept sensing was this big lady who wore a blue hat called Rose, who felt that she was fat, but it was more like she was bloated, or full of fluid. It never occurred to me that it was her condition I was picking up. I also knew that she was a prostitute. Then I was aware of a tall man who wore black, including a tall black hat, and who did not seem to like women. He belonged to a sort of secret society. And when I asked the lady about him she said yes, he was strict and very private and did not like women. He belonged to a group, a bit like the freemasons, that met at the local inn. There were many more things that were discovered about the building and all the events that we felt had happened there. It was so amazing that this woman came into the shop because she was a shy type and was not interested in beauty and had never set foot in the building since she was a little girl, even though she had always lived in the same town. What made her daughter bring her there? Why did we get the answers to the questions? It was situations like these that just kept happening and which we could not ignore.

Chapter 5

Sitting here at my breakfast bar in my kitchen, what is it that I want to say to you? What are we here for? Do we care?

I think that we have reached a point in evolution where we are able to find the answers to this question, or more to the point, are ready to ask the question. Maybe some people think that looking for our truth is just a fashion or a fad, or that there is no point because we are not able to find that ultimate truth. Ever since life began, people have been searching, and no one has ever proved it. Well, this fashion is here to stay and we're here at this time because we are now able to know more of who and what we are, so we can evolve to our next stage of being.

We are collectively beginning a journey to our true selves. And this is going to be the most rewarding and exhilarating thing you could ever imagine. Just like the song 'Imagine' by John Lennon: 'Imagine all the people living for today. You may say I am a dreamer but I am not the only one. I hope some day you will join us and the world will live as one.'

ONE! Yes, that's what I wanted to say; there is only ONE, just ONE essence. ONE Earth. ONE moment. I knew I had something to write but I did not know what, this song just popped into my mind and led me to write what comes next. This is an event that happened in my mind, which I might have ignored, but I have learnt to pay attention as every thought I have has the potential to teach me.

The Earth is divided up into trillions of different parts, from microscopic organisms to elephants. And let's not forget human beings. But when you are standing on the moon looking back at the Earth, all you see is a colourful ball. And maybe if we could sit on the outside of the universe it might be only one among many balls. This is what Einstein was referring to when he described relativity. It is perception that creates our reality, even our beliefs, depending on where you are when you perceive something and, of course, what you have been brought up to believe in. Maybe we should access all the information we have been given and see what we think about it, now that we are grown up. But where do we start?

How about at the beginning of our journey, here on Earth. Go back to your earliest memory and take a look. Remember what you thought then and see if that thought has changed. I bet you that it has. This is because you have now lived and experienced things for yourself. If it hasn't changed, consider why not. Start to form your own opinions on all things. Sometimes we simply believe things and never question them, for lots of different reasons. When I was small I believed that everything was perfect. As I grew up, people, experience or events started to show or tell me that all was not perfect. Now I am all grown up, and guess what? It is perfect again.

So here is one belief that changed and then changed back. You might ask how I can say that everything is now perfect. Well, this is because I see everything as part of a perfect plan. Just one thing moving around, being what it was always designed to be. This is perfect. Perfection is something we tend to seek or strive for instead of accepting, but by accepting we allow whatever to be what it appears to be. We seem to believe that if we reach perfection we will be happy. So we spend our lives trying to reach this perfection that will give us our happiness.

Chapter 6
Perfect

We work with a belief pattern that was set in our being by our life experiences, or other people's experiences, which they have passed on to us. The belief pattern can come from different places, via the media, books, or what other people tell us. Here are a few examples of what I am talking about:

If we exercise we will be fit and have a good life.
If we eat a well-balanced diet we will be healthy.
If we study hard we will be successful.
If we are beautiful/handsome we will have everything we need.

All of these statements are true to a certain extent, but they are not the whole truth. Each of these is trying to create perfection while telling us what it takes to be perfect. There are an equal number of negative beliefs that cause us to behave in perfection-seeking ways:

Don't smoke, you will die of cancer.
Don't drive fast, you will kill yourself.
Don't show your emotions, it is weak.
Men don't cry.

What we need to seek is our own perfection. Each of us on a physical level is very different, with different requirements. The reason behind each of these requirements is that everyone is looking for things to make them feel great. Feeling great only truly happens when you are aware that you are living according to your contract, doing what you came here to do. If you become so involved in one part of you (say, through excessive exercise), then you will become unbalanced. This is when a person can have major problems in their life. If it is not recognised, then something worse could develop. At this time, for your own good, you need to reassess your situation and what your requirements are.

When trying to connect to their essence or higher self, most people are told to do this or do that; because this was how the teachers found themselves. The reason that this way worked for them is that it was in their contract. And if yours is similar it might work for you too. So here we have human beings who have done everything that is required of them, and guess what, it did not happen. And it never will because they are following other people's ways instead of discovering their own. Life is only full of disappointment when it is not our truth we have been following. To discover what is right for you, you have to take steps in one direction or another. It will not just happen, you need to take action first. This is the road to discovery, the discovery of you. And when you discover your self as an essence you will discover how perfect you are and have always been, as a human, it is just that you have spent your time trying to be someone else's idea of perfect. So by accepting ourselves, we are more than halfway there. The other half is accepting life as it is and discovering what it is teaching us, and the magic behind it all.

Chapter 7

Remembering

Over the last year or so I have started to notice things that are so finely tuned that most of my life I'd missed them. I now know that I was simply not remembering them.

There is nothing we don't know within our inner being. We tend to think that we have discovered something new by accident, until we are able to understand it completely. This can take some time. It is only then that we realise we knew it all along, only not in a physical way. This memory is what I call pre-birth memory, it is not registered during your lifetime, it's a memory that you are a born with. It is your blueprint; it is part of your life contract. You are in the process of waking up to that secret memory.

Anyway, back to what I remembered. Each and every thing has a vibration. This vibration has a sound, a sense, a taste and a colour. A sound wave has a vibration; in the same way a colour has a vibration. Within each vibration there is another vibration which links to yet another. I can sense that I am losing you here but I will try to explain it. Each person, plant, animal or object emits a vibration because it belongs on a physical level. All material things are made up of trillions of tiny atoms that are spinning at an immense speed, faster than anything we could possibly imagine. The speed, the oscillation, and the on/off action, is what creates the vibration, which in turn produces colour, sound, smell and movement. This is our Earthbound vibration. Within and all around us there is another vibration. This is our soul vibration.

I would like to say that this soul vibration is the same in everyone but recently I have become aware that this is not the case. When I handwrote this passage on 28 February 2001, it was what I was aware of at that time. Now, as I am typing it out, the situation is slightly different. There are large groups of soul vibrations and these groups tend to attract the same vibration as themselves. The categorisation of vibration is nothing to do with the colour of a person's skin or what a person believes in or where they live. They belong to one particular set of vibrations, which seem to tune into one another, a form of attraction that is natural. Then there is another set of vibrations which all stem from one source. This source is what we call God, 'all that is' or whatever term you use to describe the starting point of existence.

There are other vibrations, which certain people such as myself experience, that vibrate at a much higher frequency. These vibrations are from a different energy field and belong to what we call higher consciousness.

Let's backtrack and start at the beginning. Let's say, for argument's sake, that there is one vibration, which we call God, love, light, or all that is. Whatever we call it, this form of energy is a powerful creative force. This force decided to create a different feeling so it divided itself into a trillion different particles, each with its own vibration to do its own set of things. Each one of these trillion particles can create its own separate set of vibrations (remember that a vibration is what creates) so each particle became a trillion particles and set off in different directions to create and then discover all kinds of things in all kinds of ways. The things that these particles created are everything that we know and a great deal more that we don't know.

So on our planet there are trillions of different vibrations all relating to a particular thing: dog, cat, flower, human. We are all made up of vibrations from the original God, all that is, as well as from vibrations from the particles that made more particles that made human beings. This is the same as what we do in our lives now; we create new things that are part of the creative vibration force (anything that is thought of, then turned into a reality through action). So within and around each human being there are many different vibrations.

My journey on this planet at this time allows me to understand a great many of these vibrations. I am able to help people discover what and who they are by tuning into their signal. When you pick up or receive information from another plane or field or existence, it comes in as a vibration. It will have a particular frequency depending on where it is coming from. The message it is giving will be a unique vibration. Now you understand why sometimes people get confused when receiving messages. They are having to interpret a whole array of vibrations at the same time, not forgetting their own. I know that this may seem off the wall, but it is the only way I can describe the indescribable.

So if we happened to find ourselves in an altered state of reality, we would communicate by picking up vibrations and sending them at the same moment, as there would be no time flow. This is achieved by being free (from our sense of self) and not thinking (which makes us a self). It is very different to what we are normally used to doing, but we have all experienced this form of communication, probably without realising it. Here is an example. Imagine you are sitting in a room and someone walks in. If what they are feeling at that moment is a strong emotion like anger, sadness or happiness, you perceive this with your sixth sense, before you have had time to think about it. You will also respond with your sixth sense and not be aware of it. So, even by doing nothing, you are giving and receiving a definite effect.

I knew that my life was changing, not so much in a physical sense, more within my mind. I was becoming aware of a whole new way of being. My mind was so much bigger and more knowing than I thought possible. This knowing was the intuitive part of my mind. I also learnt that my mind was not part of my brain as I had thought it was. My mind appeared to be a being in its own right, a separate identity to the person I knew myself as. Over time I realised that this mind was more my truth than the person I knew as Sonya. As time went by I learnt how to live this new way of discovery and inquiry and I just kept on learning and growing. This growth was not measurable to the outside world. There was no test that would show how I now knew so much more than I used to. But I did not have the need to prove my self to anyone. I knew, and that was the most important discovery I had made

We spend most of our lives learning and proving what we know to the outside world to gain recognition or acceptance. I was on the road of discovery to an inner world of humanity, which was all about personal acceptance and how to live this new way of being. Once I had discovered how life and living could be easier, then I felt this overwhelming desire to teach other people how to discover it for themselves, such a very simple way to discover their truth, as I had. What I discovered was so pure and free from any need to be known in any defined format that I had a very hard job converting this pure freedom into an understandable teaching that would be accepted.

It is easy. It is just hard learning how easy it really is.

Chapter 8
Space

Everything that exists as we know it exists in space. The space in between us, the space in which each molecule spins and the space within everything in existence. There is only one true space because there is only one thing that is. To become aware of this space is to become aware of bliss, grace, God or all that is. The way to be in touch with space is to be in the moment that it exists in, which is the Now. This Now moment is all we truly have. So each pathway, journey or religion tries to teach us to be in space, in the moment of Now. Once you are aware of this moment you are able to understand beyond that which exists within a normal level of consciousness.

In our normal reality we only pay attention to the things that are solid and can be received by our five senses. We only know something exists because we can touch it, see it, smell it, hear it or taste it. Everything we learn is based in logical thinking.

True space (which is nothingness) exists in our sixth sense. This is better described as knowing. To know something means that you are aware of it on every level of your being. To be able to get to the place where this knowing is, you have to activate your natural sixth sense. The only way to do this is to be in the Now moment. But how can we get into the Now moment?

There are many things or ways that can take people there. The easiest way is to pay attention to what you're thinking to start with. Pay attention to what you're feeling. Pay attention to what you're doing. Become aware of what is going on around you and within you. This is giving full attention to the moment you are in. Whilst this is happening, find a space where nothing is going on and nothing is happening. Here in this space is all that there is. It is here that you begin to understand on a greater level. After a period of time and with practice, you can become aware of the space. You almost see things as a flat piece of paper, or as if looking at a movie on the TV.

There are certain areas on the planet where it is easier to tune into your higher consciousness. They do not have to be historic sites such as Glastonbury or Stonehenge, although it does tend to be easier in these places because over the centuries people have given theirselves freedom there to feel and to let go, even if just for a moment. This they can do by worship, ritual or just by looking back in time and contemplating. Right where you are at this moment you can connect to your truth, you can free yourself from who you think you are and become nothing. So why aren't you? I know. Do you?

It is fear; that overwhelming sensation that paralyses us, keeps us in our body and controls our sense of self and the way we see life. The reason for this fear is a need to uphold our unique identity of separateness because we want to continue knowing ourselves as an individual; we want to continue playing our role. Most people won't even try to open their mind to the possibility of there being anything other than what they can personally experience in what they call reality. But what is reality? Anything that is proven. We all accept proof, so reality is yours to experience for yourself. You need to be free to experience what your reality is teaching you. I gave myself freedom to discover more of what I was seeing, feeling and sensing. It was only by doing this that I lost my fear of the unknown and started to discover how incredible this universe is.

Chapter 9
The Path

Life has a path, but most of the time we have to walk that path before we are aware that it has a structure and a reason. Only at the end of our journey, when looking back at it, do we see how everything fell into place. Once we become aware, once we are able to get in touch with our higher consciousness, we are able to know the path that we are walking along, its structure and reason, while we're walking along it. This information is available only through our sixth sense. This gives our self and our life more reason and understanding, which in turn helps us to lead a better life. To become aware of the path or the journey we are living is such a wonderful experience. So we now know that to get to be aware of our path we need to use our sixth sense, which connect us to our higher consciousness. To get to the moment where we start this process is different for everyone, but I have noticed that there can be a common feeling with most of the people I have worked with, they appear to reach a stage in their life, not attached to age or situation, when they ask themselves a question: What's the point?

I will explain how important this question is. As small children we reach a point when we become aware of our surroundings and start to learn how to interact with them. As we grow we learn more and more how to use this body that is us, and we learn more about what it means to be ourself. What we have learnt is great, but there is still more to learn than what we have discovered. One of the things we learn is that we are a separate being, in charge of our own body, even if we are told by our parents or teachers to do things that we don't want to, we can refuse. At this point, we gain our sense of self. We learn how to get our own way, either by being good or bad. We do not know good or bad, we are taught this, so this good and bad are set by the people in our lives. If they teach us that some things are bad, that's what we eventually learn. The more we grow, the more we learn and the more we become aware of all the things and places and differences that there are on this planet we live on. So here we are, we have quite a bit of living and learning under our belt.

The tribe that we belong to will have a big influence on what life we are going to live, so take a look at your tribe and your elders and see what they do with their lives. Now you are either going to do something similar to them or go in another direction completely. This will depend on whether you think that this type of living will suit the type of person you know yourself to be. Here you are, you have reached the point where you are free to live your life the way you want to. This is what we all do at different ages, at the moment we become responsible for our self. From this point on we are still learning and gathering what we need. You are building up a picture of the type of life you want to live. You start to recognise that all you seem to be doing is going in one direction or another, looking for this future you have been creating. When is this life you want going to start? You find a partner who suits you and you fall in love, you start your life together, yet you are still working towards a future. Then you may have children, acquire a house, a car, a couple of pets, have great holidays that show you how wonderful it is to be free from this life you have created. Whatever you seem to do there is always a point in the future that is the starting point of this wonderful life you seek. You might think it is when you can afford that next big house, or that great job, which you have worked so hard towards. You get all the things you ever wanted, that you thought would create that perfect life, and is it enough? No. When are you going to be truly happy and content? You're not. Then one day you say to yourself, What's the point????

No matter what you do, what you have, this wonderful life keeps evading you.

The whole of your life has been there to assist you to this point. You will hate the way you feel because it will show you that no matter what you do, how you do it, no matter how much you have, it is never enough. This is the saddest moment for us, it is almost unbearable.

Wake Up!!!

Yes, this is the moment you have been looking for; this is that future event you have been searching for. This is the start of the journey to the discovery of it all, the reason behind everything, everything you do and everything that is known. This is like starting all over again, only this time you are a grown-up. It is the point. At the point at which we can learn the point, by learning the secret life beyond the life you knew, you will discover your point.

When we first become aware of the bigger picture, we tend to question the purpose of continuing our journey here on Earth. Once we know our true nature in its magnificence, real life as we know it to be, is in comparison, disappointing. We can see no point to a physical life. All the things that we spend our lives searching for and believing would make us happy, we now know will fail us. It is such a shock to realise that what we were looking for, that happiness, bliss, well-being, does not exist in anything we thought it did. We had possession of it all the time.

This is stage one of the journey. We become aware of the path. We then have to learn to bring this happiness down through us and live it as much as we can. When we reach this point, life begins to be more real than it has ever been. We still do exactly the same things as before but suddenly everything has a different meaning. Our needs change; all material things take their rightful place, they cease to be a necessity for happiness. At this point of our journey we find pleasure in everything outside of ourselves, just as we always have done. Being connected to our truth takes nothing away from our lives. It is only our requirements that are different. Everything else around us has the ability to be a bonus or not. It is not essential to our inner happiness.

Chapter 10
Standing Still

Everything that exists, exists in the same space. When we experience other realms we do not go anywhere; it all happens right where we are, only our perception or our reality changes. So all that is, or all that ever can be, is only in one space and is viewed from where we are. This is hard to make clear, but I will try.

We know we can travel around our planet and beyond our planet and yet wherever we find ourselves, we are still in one space. If we are sitting in a flat in London and have an altered state of awareness, we have not moved, only our mind and awareness have changed. But at that moment we can be in any country, dimension or planet, any time frame on Earth, past, present or future.

If we were to look at life as if it were a giant book on the planet Earth and all of its existence, with trillions of stories about different people in all the different time frames, whatever page we turn to in the book, we would be where we are, in Earth time. When we experience some other realm or level of awareness, it is like looking at a book or a flat movie screen. So we know we are in some other reality and we are aware that we have not moved anywhere. We're just viewing a scene or, more to the point, we are becoming a scene. When we first connect to our inner self it feels as if we are not really there, but we are seeing where we are from a different perspective. Everything feels strange and surreal but more real than we could possibly imagine. We become aware that we are there and also not there, in the exact same space and at the same time.

It is so easy to understand when you have been there and almost impossible to explain to anyone who hasn't. But once you have started to see life in this way you realise that nothing is concrete. Everything is a contradiction, but in its contradiction it is perfect and natural. I know that if you give yourself a chance, by letting go, which will make you become free in your thoughts, this will help you to see and know more about life and yourself and you will experience the missing magic that is always there.

So there's only one space and no such thing as time because you can be in any time you choose, at any time. It is, however, time that causes us the biggest problem. When trying to describe other levels of existence, time is the main barrier that locks us away from our true selves. Time was set up for us so that we see or feel that everything is separate. Seconds, minutes, hours, days, weeks, people, plants, rocks and water appear separate because of time and space. Here is an example of time. You are reading this book in time, I'm writing it in time and it already exists in time, and I have not yet finished writing it. This is why we have such a hard TIME figuring it out.

Okay, I am now going to show how I react or see life now that I know my truth, and I hope it will help you to discover your truth.

I am free. Yes, it's that simple. I have found freedom in the chaos of life, and it only happened because I became aware of a moment in time, a gap, a space, where that thing called time does not exist. By being free I am an observer of life as well as a participant. This led me to discover so much about our identity and the way we experience everything around us. I saw where our problems lay and I knew how to solve them. This freedom was allowing me to know wisdom, a wisdom that was so simple and pure that I wondered why we made life and living so difficult.

I have broken down what I know into situations that we find ourselves in every day and have shown you how I now experience them. I hope that this will help you to grow and understand that your life and your thoughts are up to you. By changing only your attitude you will change so much.

Chapter 11
Forgiveness

In all religions we are told to forgive. But why is it so important to forgive? And what is forgiving?

Forgiving is to stop blaming, to stop blaming someone or something. We have to see things from a different point of view. If we do not forgive a person for doing something against us, what are we saying? 'I don't know why you chose to behave that way.' We have no idea why someone would behave in a certain way. We have no understanding of their reasons or motivation. Most of the time people behave badly out of fear and it is normally a response to the way they feel about themselves, nothing to do with the person on whom they inflict their behaviour. So to be able to forgive someone we must first understand where he or she is coming from on a deeper level. We can achieve this by looking at the situation as an observer, as a third party from the bigger picture. This means seeing the cause and effect of the action and its consequences, and usually, by doing this, we can see how this person's actions caused a change in us. And it might be that we needed that change.

To forgive someone, you're actually freeing yourself from his or her behaviour, dissociating and disconnecting. It is no longer anything to do with you. To forgive someone or something is not to say it's okay; it is to let go. Let go and it is not a problem any more. Letting go will free you from a mindset that can only harm you. I personally think that learning to forgive can help us move on in our lives. And once we have managed to forgive we will automatically learn about letting go. And if you learn to let go, you will know what it is to forgive.

Chapter 12
Let Go

In my work, one of the main problems I've come across with clients is that they try too hard to connect to their inner self or higher consciousness and this proves to be detrimental to the process. This applies to all situations in life, not just to this kind of work. When we feel that we are grasping at straws, trying too hard to make something work, this is when we must let go. Those two little words can have so much effect if you can really put them into action. Let go of whatever you are trying to do or whatever you are stressed about. To let go of anything implies that you were holding on. This is one of the biggest obstacles in our journey to self-realisation. Holding on to a job, a relationship or a belief, you name it, we hold on to it. The reason we hold on so tightly to things outside of ourselves is so that we can have definition; we can say who and what we are. I am a doctor, I am married, I am a Catholic, or I am right. As long as we have a title we feel that we are someone. We need to train ourselves to let go. This means that whatever the next moment is, it is free to unfold. The more freedom we allow ourselves, the more we know that we are not what we do, the better we will feel.

So let go and discover a new truth about the situation and yourself. Then, whatever the issue was, it will just drop away. You cannot hold on to it if it is not constructive. And guess what? You come back with a fresh new outlook with which you can now work, or you can simply let go again. Letting go is almost the same as freeing the spirit of self, seeing life more clearly. When we hold on to an issue, we cage up our spirit. This does us no good, on any level. By freeing ourselves, things start to fall into place. Try it, let go and let be.

Each process in the growing cycle of life has a pattern that needs to unfold when it is ready. To try to rush a stage or to help another along serves no purpose. There is always growth, so be patient with yourself and with others. The rewards are great and many. Remember that time is only of the essence that we find ourselves in, that of the human body here on Earth. The flower that fulfils its role will only bloom at the correct time. The frost might burn eager beavers. In one single day we can go from being more alive than we have ever been, to being more confused than we can remember, to trying too hard to be what we are not, to letting go and being who we were at the start of the day. If it only takes a day, an hour or one moment in time to be, then this is a truly great gift.

I find that ninety per cent of my time I am connected to my whole being. The ten per cent gets easier as I go along. It has changed from weeks of being confused and lost to only hours, which is great. I am looking forward to the time when it is minutes or, even better, only a moment or two.

We need to forgive ourselves and stop beating ourselves up for forgetting who we are. Give yourself a break and enjoy all that you have managed to do so far.

'Let go' are two words that have kept popping up in my mind and my life over the last five years. Please remember what they mean: whatever will be, will be, with no relation to the outcome. I have found that when I let go, new doors open and I see something or realise something that I had not considered before, and it is this that contributes to resolving my situation. Part of the situation may surface again, as I have already said, but if you can try to train yourself to let go when an occasion recurs, this will encourage you to go with the flow of your life, instead of getting stuck and fighting with yourself or others.

You may think that there is a contradiction here because I am not saying do nothing as your life will be the way it is designed to be. That is not what letting go is all about. We all have to be responsible for our lives and take steps to help them unfold. By letting go, we are no longer attached to the situation, and this allows us to see other possibilities that we could not see before. We are no longer caught up in the event itself.

To let go is probably one of the hardest things that we have to do on our journey because it takes faith, faith in our true self, who we have not yet met. When you manage to let go, the rewards are great, and you will be amazed at how easy it was. This is when you question why you did not do it before. Remember, to let go is to free yourself to be. This is a major part of free will: you will be free to learn, see and know. Free will is our greatest gift. To make the correct choice for ourselves we need to be free in our thinking, and the only way to achieve this is to adopt the 'let go' principle. We always have free will. At times we might think that we have no choice, but we always have a choice. There are times when we are very lost, as if we are in a black hole. This can happen in times of pain or suffering and on a physical or mental level. But it is required to assist us in our growth and learning. When suffering occurs, and as time passes, if there is no growth or no reason for the suffering, this is when we need to activate letting go. Free will is a great gift that we can know in its entirety only if we choose to use it for our growth. In other words, we need to use our free will in a positive way. Please remember that to grow is to know more of your truth. The more we get to know ourselves the easier it becomes to follow our path, and it is following your path that makes you feel complete, connected, content and loving. This is one of the main reasons for being here. We all need to find this reason at one point in our lives.

If we go through life always looking outside of ourselves for happiness and satisfaction, it will not sustain us and it will never be enough. When we discover our true nature, anything outside of us is an advantage, an extra joy, but it is not essential to our happiness. Happiness and connecting to our essence does not mean that life never goes wrong. On the contrary, life can get harder or stay the same, but it does not matter because what has changed is the way you see life. When your attitude to life changes, this is when it appears that life has changed. You see life as a bigger picture and you become an observer of your own life, as well as a participant. With this new perspective you continue to learn and grow just as before, only now you see life from a different viewing position. And believe me, it really is a great seat. Not only do you get to view yourself, you get to see behind the scenes of what makes you the person you appear to be. The beauty is that you can change the bits you don't like, but only because you were going to anyway!

The Rush

The rush of life! Are you one of those people who seeks out ways to get a rush of adrenalin? By this I mean an extreme rush, that real scary stuff! Why is it that some people take themselves to their limit and beyond? To reach your limit is to truly know yourself in a physical and mental way. To go beyond your limit is to open yourself up, which can help you to connect to your essence/soul. So to put yourself in a very scary situation and still go that one step more is daring to be. It is at that moment in time that you embrace life, discover yourself through the rush and connection of life; all alone but fully connected to something.

We do not need to base-jump, climb mountains, jump out of planes or ride roller coasters to reach this point of our existence. Within this moment of rush and connection what is truly happening is that you are LETTING GO. Yes, all it takes is to let go of fear, in whatever form it presents itself. It is the same fear that you feel when you are waiting to jump out of a plane, or when letting go of a pattern in your life: they both require a giant leap of faith. Will my parachute open? Will it change my life? Will I be happier? Is it the right thing to do? Will I land okay? Will I pass out with fear? Will I die?

So when we are at that point in our lives, when we are full of fear for whatever reason, Let Go! Once you let go you will have a rush of adrenalin to every cell in your body. At this moment you will feel so alive and so alert, more than you ever thought possible. By letting go you are free, and the rush is the reward.

Chapter 13
Free Will

I want to say a bit more about free will, which might help.

Free will is a gift, which we all possess, a gift that gives us the ability to choose. Remember that we gave it to our self. The majority of people confuse free will with will, which is easy to do, but each has a different effect on our being and stems from different layers of our self. Will is part of our Earthly human ability; it is mind/body based. Free will is within the layers of our soul/essence. Free will is the ability to be free from anything; it is a form of non-attachment. When you discover/remember who you are, then it is your free will that is activated. It allows you to be, without having to define who and what you are. When you are living your free will, you would not describe yourself as happy, sad, lonely or angry, because you are free to be whatever you require at one particular moment and free to change in the same moment. And because you know this, you have no need to know who, what or how you think you are, for you know you are all of these possibilities. This is freedom; the freedom to just be. So once you know who you are, your free will is activated.

Will, on the other hand, is used to enforce what we believe we want. We use our will to get what we want from the world around us. Will is a form of self-control that we use to manipulate others or ourselves. When we use our will, we have to back it up with control or stubbornness, and it is this enforcement that does us harm. When we force ourselves to do anything, there is always resentment attached.

You can achieve the same results with free will; only you are choosing to be, not forcing yourself to be. There is never any 'should' or 'have to' within your free will, only 'I would like to' or 'I am going to'.

You can only really know free will when you know your soul/essence. If you use it when you are not aware of your truth, then all you are doing is being lazy, using it as an excuse to stagnate. And I know this because I have been guilty of it myself.

Chapter 14
Help

There is no way that we can make someone know. We can always help someone on their journey, but they can only find knowing for themselves. I have found that the best way to help another person is to embrace your own knowing. It sort of rubs off on the people around you. By embracing your knowing, which is honouring yourself, embracing your truth, the more knowing you become. Sounds easy. Yes, it is. But for some reason we make it very hard. Maybe it has something to do with the belief that anything worthwhile is hard work.

By teaching we are naturally helping. As a teacher, I would give people the answers to their questions, even those that they had not yet asked and I would expect them to just know how easy it was. The answer might be incredible, but if they don't find it for themselves then it would have no real value to them. I had to find a way to teach that would get them to find the question, and I would then assist them in their discovery of the answer. This type of helping was constructive and productive for both parties. This is where my personal psychology came from, learning a new way of helping, and most of all letting go and allowing the process to unfold.

Chapter 15
Value

Why do we value ourselves in terms of the response of other people? Why do we look outside of ourselves to see who we are?

I would like to tell you that it is impossible for another person to value us as we can value ourselves. When another person says we are great, good looking, a good lover, a kind person, whatever term they label us with to say we are of value to the world or to them, we feel great. That same person can take it all away by one single action or remark. This will rock our world because we place who we are in their hands. There is no stability in any judgement that comes from outside of us. When we allow ourselves to be valued by someone other than ourselves, we lose.

Okay, it is human nature to want everyone to value us. Value says we are worthy of being loved. The value we need is self-value. We know we are worthy of love. So when we love ourselves, no matter what the outside world is doing, it cannot take our personal value away. And because we value and love ourselves we shine in our own honour, which will, in turn, shine through, and more people will be able to see that brilliance. They will know we're worthy of being valued and that will contribute to our knowing that we are valuable. But we will not need or rely on other people's observations of us to say what our value is.

To show your value you become valued.
To show your love you become loved.
To honour yourself you will be honoured.
To be who you are in your true light is to be the honourable,
Lovable being you are.
Me, myself and I.

I have decided to slip this passage in here for no other reason than that I could not find anywhere else to put it. It arose from a phone conversation with my sister.

It is how we see ourself that is most important to us living our truth. We cannot hide from ourself no matter how hard we try. Other people around us have their own views and you have yours. You need to really know where you are and who you are, in order to be the true person you discover yourself to be.

There are different levels or dimensions that make you the human being you are.

First there's Me, the physical person who has been running the show since I was born.

There's Myself, the part of me that has been observing the me I thought I was.

I is the essence that I know as one united front.

And Knowing is the ultimate truth. It has no definition; it has no place yet nothing can exist without it.

Then, last or first, which is neither, there is Nothing, which is, even though there is nothing, this being where 'all that is' came from, returns to but never left.

Sorry, it is confusing, but if you read this bit again it might make sense.

Within each of these parts there are many lessons to learn, and these lessons are paths to our happiness and our contentment.

The Me part is concerned with survival.

Myself is the observer of the me part and the role it is playing.

The I part relates to the bigger picture and knows what it is all about.

The Knowing part is the 'all that is', which is all that ever has been and all that could ever be. It is the totality of love, which is truth.

The Nothing is just that.

The Me, Myself and I have a job to do, and the Knowing gives the Me, Myself and I the opportunity to experience that. Remember that you are the Me, Myself and I, also the Knowing.

But most of all, the Nothing.

At this moment you probably know yourself only as the Me.

Chapter 16
Consciousness

Consciousness as we know it on a physical level is what we call reality. The consciousness we're talking about is the conscious mind or the five senses. But consciousness is a lot more than this. Consciousness of being includes the subconscious, which stores everything that we have experienced in our lives, including our dream state and the things that we don't remember in our conscious mind. It also includes the things to which we pay no attention.

Then there is our higher consciousness. This is so vast that it is impossible to define it. Our higher consciousness is aware of all that exists within our multidimensional planet, solar system, life, and all of existence. It has many different levels of awareness. Our higher consciousness is our essence, or rather an ability of our essence, just as our conscious mind is our humanness or rather an ability of our human body. The subconscious is part of both higher and Earthly consciousness; it is a link to both. As we are all playing our own unique role in this life, what we will personally become aware of on the higher levels of consciousness, the levels we will access, will be dependent on our contract, what we're here on Earth to do.

Everyone on planet Earth is on a journey that their own higher consciousness decided would benefit them most. So, depending on what our higher consciousness chose for itself to learn during its human experience, this will determine what type of life we will live. My higher conscience has decided that I'm ready, as the physical human being, to be aware of my journey and to fulfil my contract, which is to assist other people in living their contracts.

The blueprint is the soul of a person and this does not change, wherever it finds itself. Only contracts are different and changeable prior to our Earth journey. To connect to our higher consciousness we need to quieten our conscious and subconscious minds. It is then easier to pick up the vibration of our higher consciousness. This will guide your soul to fulfil the contract that you have with yourself. To quieten our conscious and subconscious minds is to be in the moment of now, as we have discussed. This can be achieved by meditation and breathing techniques, or it can just happen, as it does with me. It is paying attention to nothing, if you like. It takes time and practice to know what it is, but you will know when you are there.

Your higher consciousness can present itself to you in many different ways, depending on what you have already agreed to. I will cover this later in the book.

Chapter 17
Many Paths

There are many ways and many paths, which we all take, and each of these leads us to the next stage of our journey.

When I look back at the things that were happening to me, over the last five and a half years, they now make sense. At the time they were happening they had no rhyme or reason. I now know that I got caught up in the events themselves, instead of realising what they were trying to teach me. This does not mean I no longer get caught up in new events; I do. But I'm able to see and learn my lesson more quickly.

In the beginning, I was being shown that there is a power that is far bigger and greater than what I could ever have believed it to be. This power is who we are in our essence. We are all part of the same power ; God, Jesus, universal energy or all that is, whatever we wish to call it.

The problem lies not in what it is called; the problem is when we disassociate ourselves from It. To see ourselves as something different from all that really exists means we are on the other side of nothing, where we cannot be, because there is nothing that is not It. As soon as we realise this or wake up to our true self, we align ourselves with our contract. This is enlightenment. It should be called alignment. For this is what is required of us. We have free will to help us choose to be who we truly are. Once we become aligned or enlightened, free will changes and becomes 'all will'. What happens is that you let go of choice and life is then just what you design it to be, even though it has always been what it is supposed to be. Waking up to the truth is a part of the living process of now.

Once you have reached this awareness of your true nature, it is impossible for you to think that there is any other way to live and hard for you to believe how you used to live and see life. Then we have the hard job of maintaining this 'all that is' lifestyle because we are creatures of habit. We like to hold on to what we have always been. The tests and lessons come and go as they have always done; only now we do not get caught up in them. We observe them, learn from them and let go of them.

This journey that you are on is the journey that you chose. All that is going on in this journey is the way you chose to teach yourself to be an individual and then to discover who you really are. Take responsibility for all of you, discern and acknowledge who you are, forget who you are not. This might sound complicated at this moment in time, but the essence that is you understands what is written.

The journey of life is all about freeing you from constraints which you have allowed yourself to be put under. When you are free you have the chance to reinvent a new you. This can be achieved moment to moment, because to live true to yourself you must take each moment for what it is, not decide a moment according to a past experience. This is living in the past. This moment may seem as familiar as the past moment, but it is not, because if it were, there would be no future.

Examine the moment to reveal its truth. This way you never discriminate or take anything for granted and you allow everything to grow and change instead of being labelled.

Chapter 18
Emotions

Anger, frustration, fear, loss, depression and jealousy are some of the negative emotions that we despise ourselves for feeling. We almost feel that we are not supposed to have them, and boy do we fight them. We tend to handle these feelings a lot better if we are alone than when someone we love is around. With loved ones we dish it out in their direction, blaming them for our feelings. When strangers are around we control ourselves so as not to be judged or hated. We don't want to make a spectacle of ourselves ('should', 'ought' and 'have to' discussed later). The best place to be when we feel like this is by ourselves. Here we have no one else to take it out on. Frustration, fear and jealousy always come from that place inside us that needs to be out there in the open. After years of bottling it up inside, what happens is that one day we let it surface because we can no longer contain it. These stored emotions are cramping our growth. The most amazing thing about letting it all out is how great we can feel. I personally noticed that after a release of built-up emotion I become more receptive to my intuitive side. It is not that I am advocating feeling these emotions or saying that they help you get in touch with your intuition; what I am saying is that they interfere with your intuition. Yes, these horrible emotions that we hide are not really part of us in a true sense; they evolve from us not walking and talking our truth. We are not liars but we are guilty of denying and masking our emotions.

If we live life walking and talking our truth to the best of our ability, rather than locking away those things that bug us or make us feel bad, this helps us to be more of who we truly are. These emotions stem from hiding what we really feel.

There are, however, times of great pain, loss and suffering when we have no control over our emotions. These are true emotions that are part of our make-up and they are there to be expressed. What happens at these times is that all the other saddlebags of stored emotion come flooding out too, which can feel quite devastating. When we finally reach the stage of our journey where we are able to speak and live our truth, this is when we really start to understand ourselves and those around us. Gradually we can begin to learn to not get angry, jealous or frustrated with ourselves or other people. So embrace what you feel when you feel it and take a look at what these feelings are really saying to you.

Why am I angry? Is it because I feel I have no rights, that I cannot change things?

Why am I so frustrated? Do I think that everything that happens to me is beyond my control or that I have no choice?

What am I afraid of? Some new direction that I am not sure of, losing someone that I am very close to, or not being loved?

Once you look at what is causing these emotions in you, then you can take steps to change what you need to. I am not saying that it is a good or a bad thing to feel angry, frustrated, jealous or fearful. But do check out why you feel like this, so you can help yourself, which will also have an effect on others. This leads to a balanced life.

The night of my thirty-seventh birthday I was the most angry I can remember ever feeling, yet there was nothing I could think of that could have caused that intensity of anger. Now when I look back I know what happened. I realise that it was a trivial thing but it had the most drastic effect on my being. I thought it was my haircut but it wasn't. I didn't like my haircut; the problem was that I did not have the guts to say so. I was not speaking my truth. To make matters worse, I gave the girl a five-pound tip. The ironic thing was that I was rewarding someone for doing something I really did not like. How bizarre was this situation? It was only when I 'let go' that the pressure subsided. It was part of my truth that was breaking free that night, and it has been my truth that has been breaking free ever since.

Chapter 19
Should, Ought, Have To

Should, ought, have to. These are small words that have the most drastic effect on our lives.

They all imply that there is something we should be doing or some way we should be behaving. This in turn implies that it is a rule, it does not allow choice. All of these words are part of a process of programming that we have learnt or been brought up to believe in. They are 'controlling'. What would happen if we didn't do what we think we should? We would be free to choose (free will), not should have, ought to or have to.

Remember, this does not mean that we would not do the same things, just that the pressure is off. The fact that we can choose creates freedom. Just for one day, try to let go (those two little words again) of should, ought and have to. You can replace these words with like to, want to or even don't do. The most amazing thing happens. You free yourself from the constraints you or society has placed on you.

Okay, you lazy people out there. You might think that this is really easy, but remember that part of doing nothing is, in itself, a rebellion against should, ought and have to. So when you are free to do what you want, the story changes. Whenever we say we should, we automatically feel guilt, and guilt is detrimental to the soul. We have a great need to free ourselves from our self-control. We all have a natural sense of control that is distorted and changed when we enforce society's idea of control. It suppresses our natural nature and replaces it with a resentful, unhappy robot, automatically performing for the masses. In most situations, it will only be the words themselves that change, but when you say to yourself that you want to, rather than you have to, there is an effect on the way you feel.

There are many times in our lives when we find ourselves with certain things that we need to do, although we would not chose to do them just then. This is responsibility. And responsibility comes from choices, which we made at an earlier time on our journey. This can be a difficult situation. For example, it could be that you had a baby because you felt pressured and are now resenting all the hard work that comes with the child. The work that comes with having a child is not the child itself. There are always ways to make life a little easier. When we change our attitude towards anything it changes the way we feel. We are responsible for our lives and those of our children. It is better to enjoy these responsibilities than resent them, or try to run and hide from them.

Maybe the problems arise because we are trying to be what other people want us to be, or what we think is expected of us. When we learn to live our own lives and take responsibility for our choices, everything fits into place and we start to see how much easier it is to be ourselves. The next time you say I should, I ought or I have to, ask yourself – is this for me, or is this for someone else? Do I feel like doing this? Is this part of my picture? Am I making this a problem with my attitude? What happens if I don't do this?

Choose your life and your response to it. Be responsible for the choices that you have made and look at them with fresh eyes.

My grandmother was in a really nice nursing home but I hated seeing her there, even though I was the person who pushed for her to be there in the first place, to relieve the stress and take the pressure off my mother, who medically was not fit enough to take care of my grandmother. I felt I had to visit her, but as soon as I got there I wanted to leave, so one day I decided that I would not go until I felt that I really wanted to. Two weeks went by before I went again. In the beginning I did feel guilty, but I soon noticed that if I went only when I wanted to, my gran seemed to enjoy my company more and I wanted to stay with her longer. After I 'let go' of 'should, ought, and have to', it really did turn into 'want'. I was running away from a truth that I was not willing to look at. Life was better for her there as well as for my mother.

When she was ninety years old my gran had kidney failure and they told us that she would not live much longer. At this time, I had this feeling inside that she would die on a special day at the age of ninety-three. They had taken her off all her medication, which she had required to keep her well and living for the last thirty years. The only thing she was taking was half an aspirin a day. So in theory she was only expected to live about six weeks, not three years. But these facts did not stop me telling my mother and my two sisters what I thought.

On one visit I walked into her room and saw that she looked dazed and a bit shocked. I knelt down by her side and asked if she was okay. She said, 'Oh yes, duck,' her favourite saying. 'I have just come back.' I asked where from, knowing that she had not been out of the nursing home. She started having a conversation with me about where she had been and who she had seen. It was the most coherent she had been in years. The conversation we had was all about another dimension. I was experiencing my surges of energy and I was fully aware of where she was. This was the first time I had experienced someone else's journey into other dimensions and it was beautiful. Yvette, my younger sister, as with me and she was taken aback by the connection between us, and how the two of us seemed to be cocooned in a tunnel of energy.

On the night she died we were all there: my mother, Karen, Yvette and myself. It was an incredible night. We all knew it was the last night we would spend with her. Most of the time she was not conscious. We sang lots of songs for her, and at one point she woke up and asked me to tell them to stop singing. We all laughed.

In the early hours of the morning I saw two vibrating diamond-like shapes in the room. I blinked and rubbed my eyes, but they were still there. I knew that these sparkling prisms were energies that had come to assist her. She died slowly, and just before she took her last breath I climbed onto the bed and held her in my arms. I knew I had a choice at that moment, either to see death the way I had in the past or to let go and learn something new. At the point that her heart stopped beating this overwhelming sense of freedom rushed over me. I joined her in that moment and felt her acceptance of death. I knew I had left behind my fear of death and gained so much. The date was 29 February 2000. She was ninety-three years of age, and it was the first leap year of the new millennium. Quite a special day, eh!

The night before I had my first experiences, the night of my thirty-seventh birthday, my anger was so overwhelming that I could have driven my car into a brick wall. I made a choice. I chose life. The night my nan died I had the same choice. I chose death. The first choice freed me, which allowed me to truly begin to understand life, the second allowed me to truly understand death. I have a great respect for dying and suffering but that final act of the last breath I do not fear. And I look forward to that first breath we take every morning.

Chapter 20

Guilt

The one feeling that truly stops us in our tracks. But where does guilt come from? It comes from our mind or our actions. We are responsible for what we do; guilt is normally felt if we feel that we were wrong. There is no problem with being wrong and recognising it. Guilt is a result of doing nothing about it, or continuing doing or being what we know is wrong in our truth. We never feel guilt if our actions are perceived as wrong by other people, but not by ourselves.

So guilt is about not learning or not being big enough to say sorry and about denying our truth. There is a guilt that people feel because of situations that are out of their control, such as when someone dies. If a personal situation between two people is not resolved before one of them passes away, then the living person carries the guilt of failing to resolve the situation in time. In these situations it is not our fault that the other person died, and please remember that we can always talk to them even if they are dead. Energy is always connected.

Most guilt comes from the action or words of others being directed at us personally or via a third party. Their intention is for us to take responsibility for our deed and relieve them of their anger (justification). If we respond for their sake, we will forsake our truth and will be caught up in should, ought and have to.

If you have felt that there is nothing that you can do to make it right, then you need to let go. If you don't, you will stagnate. Your guilt may even consume you.

What sits behind this guilt is fear, and fear is this planet's obstacle to be overcome. You will never find happiness in fear; you will never find freedom, which is what allows happiness to be felt. And you cannot discover your truth through guilt or fear. There are plenty of situations in life where fear is good for us, but only as a protective instrument, not as a lifelong companion. Face your guilt head on and discover the fear or mistake behind it, then deal with it and finally let it go and give yourself a chance at happiness.

Chapter 21
Happy

For us as human beings to be happy and content generally requires many different physical, mental and emotional happenings. When we look at life from a soul level, we discover that happiness is what we are, not a requirement, as it is for us on the Earthly plane.

If we look at the physical level, we tend to consider that to be happy we need to be healthy, loved, maybe even rich or famous. What we really need is to live our truth and to be ourself. Of course, we need food and water and a certain amount of money. But whether we are a poor person living on the streets or a rich person living in Beverly Hills, our happiness depends solely on our point of view, which creates our attitude. When we look at a person living on the streets, we are thankful that we are not them or in their situation. But have you ever considered that some of those people living on the streets are looking at you, with your very full, busy lives, and thanking god that they are not part of the rat race that you are in? Of course, there are people living on the street that would much rather be somewhere else, as there are those living in a mansion in Beverly Hills who would also rather be elsewhere. You can be as lost in your riches as in your poverty. This is more apparent when we look from a soul level of awareness.

Okay, you find this a harsh view and you are probably feeling sorry for the person suffering on the streets, and maybe not for one moment would you care about the person in Beverly Hills. But, on a soul level, prior to our Earth life, we decided what we wanted to experience and the best way for us to achieve that in order for us to find ourselves.

Buddha was no different from a man living on the street. He relied on other people's generosity to feed and clothe him, but did not rely on anything other than himself to make him happy, because he had found the secret to life. His happiness came from knowing who he truly was, as an essence.

So on a physical level we most certainly need food and water to give our bodies energy, and we can only get this energy from the land.

We all need a certain amount of money, although perhaps not as much as we think. It might be in our contract that we need large amounts of money to learn the energy of money and what we can achieve or not achieve with it. Without money there would be no growth in technology or science, which would halt discovery. Things would not be invented or created to make our lives easier, which, in turn, supposedly allows us more time to discover ourselves. So thank you, money.

Without money we would not have all the things that technology has produced and we would not have to spend time looking after them and having to work hard so we can replace them when they are dated or broken. If we have none of these things that money can buy, then we have so much more time in which to get to know ourselves. So thank you, money.

Either way, money has the ability to teach us to see and recognise ourselves beyond it.

Love on a physical level can have a similar effect. When we have a loving relationship with another, it fills our time and makes us feel great. When we don't have a loving partner, we spend most of our time looking for one. This searching can feel good or bad, depending on how we see life. The thought of something can almost be as rewarding as the achieving of it. Thought is the creative power that influences everything that is, has or could be. It is the driving force of your being. All we need to do is to use our thoughts in a direction that leads us to be who we are designed to be and enjoy being that person.

If you discover things about yourself that you don't like, change them until they truly represent you. Your true nature is when all aspects of you are in line or balanced, not being one thing or another, just being able to be anything you want to be at a particular moment. This is a balanced life, sitting right in the middle, ready to be at any moment what you choose to be. It feels like nowhere land. It's easy to make a decision from here, as it has no complexities. Sitting in nowhere land will only make sense to you when you have experienced it for yourself. What it really feels like is pure or unconditional living, which in terms of a physical Earth experience feels a little like pure unconditional love. It is so beautiful. So happiness sits in your mind, and you know that at any moment you have every possibility to be who you came here to be.

Chapter 22

Set in Stone

What I'm going to say now will appear to be a complete contradiction to the last chapter; in truth it isn't. The life we are living, as I have said, is by design, so what will, could and has happened to you is not changeable. So, in truth, you could and will only live the life you are living. It is the way that you feel and respond to life that is up to you. We have free will, but not how we think. Yes, I am saying that your life is mapped out for you and you cannot change it. You created it for yourself to give yourself an opportunity to learn. The learning is within this human existence you find yourself in, which is also experienced by the other levels of you.

You have a destiny that is set in stone. Therefore you will live the life that you require. Remember, the part of you that created the person you are now knows life and existence to be something completely different to what you are aware of at this moment. Putting it in simple terms, your soul wrote the movie that you are now acting in. The movie can only be what is written (your contract). The character you are playing is evolving and has done from the moment you were born, owing to your interaction with other souls on the planet. When you wrote this movie, it was a mass of energy (your soul) that had a thought. This thought was transformed into a reality (your life).

But that thought/movie is the whole planet Earth's existence, from start to finish. Yes, there is an end. Now, imagine watching a movie that is set in different times in our history, jumping from the big bang to the final big bang, with billions of different lives and situations in between. This is a long movie! But this is how life on Earth appears to our essence. It was created from a thought and turned into a reality using an aspect of our essence to create a soul, in turn becoming zillions of aspects of soul. These aspects of soul are everything in creation on our planet. So, if you become aware of there being no such thing as time, which happens when you discover the moment of now, you understand that this is all happening in the same moment. So, then, what has, could or ever will be on this planet has been and gone in a moment. Sorry, but in truth we are an illusion that believes it is a separate identity, because that is all it knows itself as. That is, until it discovers its secret truth.

So, your soul is playing many parts in the Earth movie. What I am saying here is that it would be the same as your thoughts being aware of themselves, also being able to think and believing that they exist and that they are the truth. Even if a lot of those thoughts are turned into condensed matter and have a reality, they are not the truth. They are a function of your brain that you turned into an object, by creating in time and space. Yes, we are a living thought that thinks for itself and, as a result of this thinking, we then have reason. It is that reason which leads us to try to discover where we came from.

At this moment, all my thoughts are trying to figure out where they came from. If they had this ability, and they discovered that they were not real, they would understand that they are in fact a part of this thing called a brain, which sits inside this mass, that sits inside these layers and layers of substance. The more they discover, the more they realise that they are part of this whole existence. They will reach a point where they realise that without them (thoughts) there is no existence.

So even though they have discovered that all they are is a 'thought' that happened in a moment, and that was all, they go back to enjoying being a 'thought', knowing that being that 'thought' allowed them the opportunity to discover their truth. And because there is also so much more that they could be when it is over, they are happy to be.

Chapter 23
Creativity

Happiness is a state of being. This means that we are very happy to just be. But in order to know that we are being, we need to measure ourselves against something. So this whole world out there is our measure.

I hear it all the time from different people; they say that they are not creative. It is their idea of what this means that stops them knowing how creative they are. Their creativity comes from their representation of their unique self, measured by being and doing on this planet, not by their ability as compared to others'. It is the mark that we leave where we have been that says we were there, that is creativity. So anything we do or are on this planet is creative. The more we leave our mark, the more we feel that we have achieved. There are different levels of being creative that are only recognised in comparison to other abilities. 'She is a great singer, he is a great artist, the best cook ...' This is comparing them to the abilities of others. But true creativity is being free to express our uniqueness, and the more we do this, the happier we feel. This is because our happiness is in being fully present while doing, and the reward is achievement, not recognition. I enjoy interior design, I love finding different things in different shops and creating a picture in one of the rooms in my home. When the room is finished, I stand back and admire my creation, and I think how great it was to be able to put this all together and express what I like. If other people like what I have done, it feels nice, but if they don't, I don't care because I was doing what I enjoyed and it felt nice to me. I don't need to be recognised by anyone else to be happy with what I have achieved. I have this same feeling in most of the things I do when I really put myself into it, whether I am cooking, doing a piece of artwork, cleaning a room or writing a passage in my book – the pleasure and the happiness come from being fully present in my creative representation of Sonya.

Chapter 24
Energy

The energy that is 'all that is' is neither positive nor negative – it is just pure potential energy. But potential energy does not exist as a format, it awaits and is within everything and is everything. It is there for us. The gift that we all have of free will is the ability to use this energy in any way that we choose (within the terms of our contract).

No expectation comes from the energy; it is always the same. With free will we can choose to fulfil our contract in either a positive or a negative way. Either way, we will complete our contract. Someone choosing to use the energy in a negative way will prove how not to live in a particular way. Lesson learnt, hopefully. People's negative actions can have a remarkable effect on other people by teaching them how not to do certain things. Some negative actions can achieve positive results in the short term, which can encourage other people to do the same. I have learnt, after years of experiencing and looking at positive and negative actions, that the end results can appear to be exactly the same. So why would we bother to choose or consider a positive way?

Energy is pure essence, so when we achieve something in a positive way we get the pleasure of feeling that true pure energy, and it is this connection that spurs us on. Over time, this lifts our self to a level that is closer to our truth. A negative approach does not have this effect, but I want you to remember that without negative energy there is no learning to be had. This planet is made up of opposites, and without one, the other does not know itself. You are going to live the life that is yours because, remember, it has already happened.

We have a contract to fulfil, or, more to the point, a life to live. Why not have all the pleasure from fulfilling your contract the way you are designed to? There is a feeling inside us all, that we are here to do or be a particular thing. The closer we get to that particular thing, the better we feel about ourselves. This is when we know we're doing exactly what we came here to do, being exactly who we came here to be (not that we could be or do anything different). It is a sign that we are on our way to our truth. The best way to live the life you came to live is with a positive attitude. This is a big part of your life and contract. The best way to live the life you came to live is with a negative attitude. This is a big part of your life and contract. That has a thrown a spanner in the works! But it is true. Remember that there is only one and, for anything to exist, it is always going to be a part of the one. For us to accept the truth we need to understand it, and to understand it we need to view it from a distance. The only way that this is possible, while still being a human being, is to use our mind. Our mind has the ability to connect us to our higher consciousness, even though they are one and the same. From this connection, we are aware of our truth and the reason for this truth. As humans, we cannot easily accept this truth. It goes against the principles that govern us; because what I am saying here is that God and the Devil are ONE. Any philosophy or religion that says that there is a creator is saying the same as I am. The illusion is that both of them exist as entities, they only exist because of our need to know there is a greater power. There is no way in truth (knowing) that part of itself can be anything other than its self. The only way is to set up an illusion that is so good that the illusion believes itself to be a self. A human being.

Chapter 25

Intuition

One or two people have told me that they followed their intuition and yet look where it got them. Where they are now, for some reason or another, feels bad. Well, maybe that is exactly where they are supposed to be, so that they are able to learn something that they need to know for a current, future or even past event. If where they are is not right for them, they have free will to change it at any time, which will allow them to see the same situation differently. It might be that they were precisely where they were meant to be to learn how to use their free will, in the first place. Sounds crazy, I know, but life teaches us in many ways. It also teaches us to take steps instead of just drifting. So move - don't stand still until you stagnate.

Life has many possibilities, but to know what is right or wrong for us, we have to make decisions or take steps in one direction or another. Once we have chosen a direction and have put things into action, we will be right where we wanted to be. If this does not feel right then we can make another choice. It is by taking steps and deciding one way or another that we are helped to discover our true nature.

Free will is a gift that we chose for ourselves to enable us to learn all about who we are and who we are not, but not only in our everyday moments. It is our secret tool that helps us to discover our truth. So use it.

In today's world, we are so concerned about making mistakes that half the time we forget to live. Once we discover our true nature, we very rarely need to make choices. Because we know ourselves, it is more like us going along with the flow of life. Things that used to bother us cease to do so. Once we are aware that we are on our path, we will have a greater understanding of the journey that brought us there. We become aware of our intuition and how it really works, and discover that it was helping us all along. It was never wrong.

Who and what we are is very personal, and sometimes we forget this fact. And because we forget, we then ask other people about who and what we are. And they only know you as the you which you are presenting. So unless you are living your truth, the people around you will never be able to say who you are.

I have just been on the phone with two friends of mine who are trying to make a life together, trying being their main problem. They are both intuitive and the lady has had many more experiences of what it is to live your truth. Their relationship is at breaking point, as it has been many times before. They really do love each other but they cannot find a balanced life together or apart. That is why they keep coming back to each other. Now they either have something to learn that they are not paying attention to or they are going to manage to make this relationship work. When I advise them I ask them to do what is right for themselves. Honour the persons they are and let go of the issues that are stopping them living their truths. If they manage to do this then they could either have a really great relationship or go their separate ways, making space in their lives for someone else to love. Remember, it is fear that sometimes stops us from taking action in a direction we know we need to go. But normally when we love a person we think that we have to make it work. I believe that they feel resentment for each other because they want each other to be the type of person they know they can be. The person they truly like in each other is the essence, but neither of them can let that shine through them for long periods of time. They don't like quite a bit about the persons that they used to be, before they discovered more of their selves. So they are fighting that part of each other. Then they make up and try to do what the other person wants. Which is not living your truth. All I can do is to encourage each of them to be true to their self and allow their journey together to unfold. Whether they stay together or not is not what is important here; but being who they are discovering their selves to be is. This may go against the normal way of helping, but it really does work, and whether relationships improve or break up, either way it is for the best. There is never any point trying to be someone for someone else. You will only end up resenting and blaming them for all your problems. Take responsibility for your life and your journey and live it in away that allows you the freedom to express the incredible being you are.

The closer you are to your truth the more you naturally want to share your love and life with other people. You don't do it to please them so they will like you more, you do it because it lifts you and makes you happy. As for what will happen with my two friends, that is up to them.

When we learn that we are more than what we think we are, it takes time and practice to allow this bigger part of us into our every moment, and this is where my two friends are at this juncture. The only way to maintain your truth is to live it.

Chapter 26
Taste

Taste - this is what we like or enjoy, and it is a very personal sense. For some reason, we seem to let other people influence our personal taste. Why? It can only happen when we are not sure of ourselves. If we participate in something that we enjoy, find fulfilling and are truly passionate about, we do not let the attitudes or opinions of other people affect us. It is when we are not sure about ourselves, or of a particular thing we are doing, that we allow the opinions of others to influence ours. The only way to resolve this is to ensure that everything you do is right for you and that it reflects your being. It is not about someone else; it is your taste, your life. If we do not put all of ourselves into what we are doing, then it is not a true reflection of us. We need to live consciously, in the moment that we find ourselves in, and then the opinions of others are disconnected from us. It does not mean that we will not be considerate of other people's opinions, rather that we will not allow them to have an effect on our own taste, unless we choose to.

You know the saying 'He is sure of himself'. This is what I am talking about here; being sure of yourself and your taste, by giving whatever you do your full, conscious attention. This is called confidence. You are perfectly designed for the role you are playing in your movie and have all the tools and the ability to use them. Once you discover this truth about yourself, your life will become your own, which in turn will give you a better understanding of others and an acceptance of their individual taste, which of course will rub off on them (cause and effect).

Chapter 27

Information

There are times when we receive new information intuitively. We are aware of the change although we can only sense it. We know that we know something, but to try to find a space for it to exist within our normal logical thinking brain seems impossible. There is a process that happens when we receive new information, or should I say remember something. This process is quite strange. It starts with knowing, which sits in our higher consciousness; then this knowing has to be adapted (stepped down) until it is understandable on a normal conscious level - in other words, so we can understand the information through feelings or taste or symbols such as words and pictures. It is like reducing the voltage of electricity until it is safe to use. For our own use, the stepping down is not necessary, but to be able to pass on what we know to other people, the information needs to be converted and articulated.

At this present time, I am experiencing this process. A week ago, I was talking on the telephone when a powerful feeling came over me. It was so powerful I could not speak, even greater than most of the surges I have experienced, and boy, have I experienced some powerful events. It was like a wave of powerful energy engulfing me. In those few moments, which seemed like a lifetime, it removed the entire past – not only mine, but the entire history of Earth – and there was a feeling of no future. It was not like enlightenment or being there in the moment, yet it was similar to these experiences. The only way I can describe it is to say that I moved into a fifth-level dimension while still existing in the third and fourth dimensions. Time and space are the fourth dimensions, and I am referring to dimension not as a measurement but as a law of existence. Although we already exist on all levels and in all dimensions, for me it was as if the veil between the fourth and the fifth had been lifted.

I am so aware of new information but unable to express it on a physical third-dimensional level. What I know for sure through this process is that now is the time frame that we need to get the ball rolling and take our place in the world. By being aware of the person and the place that we find ourselves in, we will feel more connected to our being.

No 'should' or 'ought' dilemmas, just 'being you', living your movie/life, which you created and continue to co-create with the bigger part of you, your higher consciousness. This is what is called walking, talking and living your truth. To do this we need to know who we are. There are ways and means that can help us to achieve this. A good place to start is to look closely at our personal history. When looking back on our own journey through life, we see what it has been saying to us, what lessons we have learned, and what appears to be our fate or destiny. If a pattern keeps repeating itself in different situations, then there is clearly a lesson to be learnt. Remember that we never stop learning, which creates growth. The true being that we are is multidimensional, so there are many levels of learning to be experienced.

All of our life has contributed to our being where we are at this precise moment. When something happens in our life that we don't understand, we must take a more analytical look at it to see exactly what is being presented to us. This entails checking it out on all levels and from all angles. Sometimes the evidence is patently obvious, whereas at other times it is interwoven with many other issues that we have not let go of, which may well take a lot of unravelling. Please don't regard this as only another mundane chore; the truth is that we gain a great deal of pleasure in finding ourselves. I know, now, why I was so full of information that I have not yet stepped down to the physical level. I have been reminded of patience, and that there is a time and place for everything - I deal with time and place in a later chapter - and that life is far more structured and organised than we think.

Six months after my first set of experiences, I asked a friend of mine from school, Eamon, to come and see me at the shop. He was the guy I had called in before, when we were hearing all the different noises and experiencing the strange feelings in the building. At this second meeting, he said, 'I told you you would be doing this type of work.' I had forgotten that he had told me this. He went on to say that the energy that I was connected to was way beyond anything he was working with. He was pointing with his left hand up to the sky. He used his right hand to point out to the side of him and show me the energy he was connected to. He also told me that my life would settle down and that most of the work would be done in a dream state. I was relieved about this, because at the time I was so scared of all the different experiences I was having. They made me feel very small in the scheme of things and totally out of control of my own life. There were many other things that we discussed – about what I was here to do and how I knew how to read people's blueprints and contracts. When he said this, I knew exactly what he meant. I did not know this logically, but deeper within my body. I am now aware that the blueprint is connected to the soul. Our soul has (or more to the point is) a blueprint that contains all of the experiences it has had (remembering that life has happened in a moment). The contract is our role as an individual human being. A contract is experiencing one of the blueprints of the soul.

About six weeks later, I went to bed as usual. It was an ordinary night and I felt far more settled. At the point of drifting off to sleep, the place I call slumber, a strange feeling rushed over me. I could smell the most revolting smell, a decaying stench. There was a high-pitched sound in my ears, almost a ringing and a whistle combined. My heart started pounding and there was this red square that was as bright as a laser beam in front of me. Even though my eyes were closed, it was as if I was still seeing. This was all happening at the same time. This overwhelming feeling of being crushed began; it was as if I was in a giant vice. I thought that I was having a heart attack and I tried to wake Ivan up but I couldn't move. I remember having had this feeling before, when I was pregnant with my daughter, only this time it was not going away. I was scared, the most scared I have ever been, and there was nothing I could do. I couldn't talk or move. It was over for me, I was dying. At that moment, I let go. I had no other option. What happened next was so mind-blowing that it couldn't be possible. The room went black, blacker than I had ever experienced before, so black that it was alive. Then the crushing sensation stopped and it felt as if I was being transported at such a high speed that lights were streaking past me. The sound was whooshing past me at high speed too. I was going somewhere, but where I had no idea. I could not believe how calm I felt. There was this warmth all around me, as if I was in the most wonderful place. This was all happening in a split second, but it felt as if a long time had passed. There seemed to be two parts of me that were aware of what was happening, the real me and a freer me, which was knowing and had great wisdom. I felt such comfort. The free me was aware that time was not passing, but that life was forever. It came to an abrupt end and then I was sitting up in my bed with my eyes open. I wondered what had just happened to me, and then all of a sudden the wall at the end of my bedroom opened up, as if it had just burst open. It was a hole about the size of a car tyre. The colour inside this hole was intense, electric and blue, a blue that was pure and real. It was not a blue we are used to seeing. It was almost too powerful to look at. There was this noise, which sounded like a party or a large gathering. I could hear glasses chinking, as if people were toasting something. Then a black man's face appeared in the hole, which made me jump. I felt as if I had just jumped out of my skin, only at this moment I was not contained within my skin. The black man had a familiar, very jolly round face with a silver-grey beard and hair. He was looking straight at me. I knew he was showing me something and I remembered what Eamon had told me about me working in dream state. So I paid full attention to what was going on. Then another black man appeared; only he was not facing me. He was younger. This scene disappeared and I saw an older black lady, who had the brightest short red hair I had ever seen. She was wearing gold earrings and was attractive. Then she disappeared and a younger black lady took her place. They were all very happy and seemed to be celebrating something, but what it was, I had no idea. Before me were two hands shaking, and I remember thinking that they must have made a deal. At this very same moment, I was patted on the head by a hand so big that it covered my whole head. I was in shock and very scared about being touched, because in reality I knew that there was no one standing next to me. I just wanted to hide, shrink or scream my head off. Then, just as quickly as this had all came about, it changed, and with a flash and a whooshing sound I was back in my body.

I was lying face down, just as I had been before anything happened. I was so exhausted that I just collapsed into a heap and fell asleep. For how long, I don't know. I woke up and it was still dark. I woke Ivan up and told him about the incredible thing that had just happened to me. He was still half asleep, yet I asked him to come down stairs with me. I had a desperate need for a cup of sweet tea to give me some energy.

He said, 'Don't be silly, go by yourself.' I told him how scared I felt and he responded by telling me to face my fears. I swore at him, pulled the covers back and stomped across the bedroom, making as much noise as possible. I had to walk past the part of the wall that had opened up and I was frightened that I might be sucked into it! I found the courage and got myself downstairs as quickly as I could. Boy, I can move when I have to! I opened the lounge door and something shot up in front of me. I screamed and literally wet myself with fear. It was my dog! She was sleeping on the sofa, even though she was not supposed to. This was my most frightening experience since that night in my conservatory, and yet it was so amazing. I knew I had travelled somewhere, but I was aware that I was still in my bed. What the message was I still don't know, but it sure got my attention. Trying to sleep that night was so hard. I felt that my whole life had been invaded and there was no part of me that was safe from this invasion. But I also knew that this experience felt more real to me than the real life I knew. I was not dreaming, but the reality I found myself in was within another realm or time. The harder I tried to make sense of this, the less sense it made. There were two sides to me; one that accepted and knew this, the other that fought it and did not accept it. This was such a powerful event that I could not let it go, but I also found it hard to live with. I had to find a solution to this somehow, and that. eventually, was simply to let it go.

Two weeks later, I had another experience in that state between sleep and being awake (the twilight zone). Believe me, it was starting to feel as spooky as the programme used to be. This time, I felt my body vibrating faster and faster. It was like a surge of energy but it didn't stop. I was aware consciously that I was entering a different space. It just was so crazy and yet it made sense to me. I knew I was going somewhere, but I also knew I had not moved. At night, I regulate my body heat with my feet. If they are the right temperature, then I can get to sleep. This night, I was too hot, so I put my feet out from under the bedcovers to cool down, as I usually did. All of a sudden, someone grabbed hold of my ankle and started pulling me out of bed. My heart was pounding in my throat and I couldn't scream. I was holding on to the edge of the bed as tight as I could. I was so terrified; what could I do, what could anybody do? I just wanted someone, anyone, to help me. I knew I was not dreaming. I opened my eyes and to my surprise I was lying on my side. Both my hands were under my chin and at the same time I felt that I was holding on to the top of my bed, lying on my front. It's OK, I'm safe, I thought, it's my spirit body that is being pulled, not my physical body. Then I could feel the hands that were pulling me out of the bed. They were so large that the span was from my foot up to my knee, and they were very soft, as if they were composed of pressurised air, not flesh and bone. There was a sense of humour about this, as if they were pulling my leg, but I was certainly not laughing. Then, just as quickly as it all started, it stopped. I woke Ivan up and told him I had had another experience and to ask me about it in the morning, as I was far too exhausted to talk now. What was noticeable about these experiences was how much energy I used up when having them. It made me feel as if I had been working non-stop for days. Another thing I had noticed was that even though I was terrified, I was also calm and accepting, and again it was showing me that there appeared to be two of me in the same body. I knew that there was nothing I could do to stop these things from happening to me and no one else could help me either. I just had to accept it and find out what was behind them and what it wanted.

Chapter 28
Thoughts

Thoughts create. That may be hard to conceive, but if I put it in simple terms maybe you will understand what I mean. I am not implying that you are simple; I simply mean that I will try to explain it in a clear and concise way.

When you think (creation) of a particular thing, such as an event, job, idea or situation, then you take action (doing) that takes you to that particular thing. By taking action you create that thing.

Now it gets a little complicated. Every thought you have is created on another level of awareness, but not as a physical thing, more like a carefree, floating possibility, which can easily materialise at any time. It is also possible for another human being to receive this thought and put it into action. Where do you think that some of your own thoughts have come from? Out of the blue, where thoughts come from in the first place? Thoughts are part of original creation. But where do they originate? Where did the thought that I would write a book come from?

I would have to say from me, but if I really think about it long and hard, it is clear that it entered my mind from somewhere outside of me. Then this thought was presented to me again through a medium, when I went to a session that Julie, my friend, had treated me to for my fortieth birthday. If you were to go and see a medium or clairvoyant, he or she would be able to see thoughts as real things. Are these thoughts your own, from someone who has passed over, or are they original thoughts? The thought that you have can be based on many things. Some thoughts we create because of things that are happening to us at that time. Whether good or bad, these are Earth thoughts. Then there are the thoughts that just slip in, as if they had nothing to do with us; they can come from universal energy that we have tuned into, from other people's thoughts or other entities. This is also why some people have a great idea and do nothing about it, only to discover a few months or so later that their idea has been put into effect by someone else.

There are also the thoughts that are part of our movie show. You will recognise these as "knowing" when you start to pay attention to them. Then they will make sense to you because they are exactly what you wrote into your movie called life.

If you have been to see a medium or fortune-teller, the information they pass on to you can be amazingly relevant or utter rubbish. The reason for this is thoughts and free will. There are creative thoughts all around you and within you. If you do not turn these thoughts into action, you would say that the fortune-teller was wrong and talking a load of rubbish. Remember that some of these thoughts did not belong to you in the first place. If you did turn your thoughts into action then you would say that the fortune-teller was great and she or he was spot on.

The more you live your truth, the more your thoughts are in line with your future events, so therefore the better the reading would be from the clairvoyant or medium, assuming that they are being true to themselves and interpreting what they receive precisely. The fortune-teller is only as good as you are at living your thoughts, so be aware of what you think!

Thoughts on a psychic level will become a reality on our level. On an Earth level, we will be required to take action for them to be transformed into a reality, but a thought that is thought over and over again is probably going to be created anyway, because it is meant to be (our contract). Thoughts on any level are so powerful that they can materialise, with enough energy (life force) behind them – just look at planet Earth. There is an old saying: 'Be careful what you wish for'.

Fortune-tellers, mediums or clairvoyants can also tell of past events that were thoughts, some of which materialised and some of which did not. The access that the fortune-teller has to your past, present and future events is the same access that you have; she has merely tuned in to another level of your being. If you tune in to yourself, you would be better than anyone else at telling your future, past or present events.

Past and future events are not static – they are as changeable as your thoughts of them. Take a past event and look at it from a different angle and it will change, maybe only slightly, but that is enough to have a major effect on things that came before and after that event. We are who we perceive ourselves to be at any given moment, so change your perception and it changes you. So now we have our original plan or journey (our movie), which we thought of and brought into action. These original thoughts were the broad basic ground rules, which, by the way, a good fortune-teller or you can read. We then become part of that living thought and we are able to add new thoughts at all times because we co-create with our free will. So where you are at this moment is the result of thoughts on many levels materialising into reality, as we know it on a physical level.

Thoughts are powerful, but it is the intention behind the thought that is the driving force or constructive part. A lot of the thoughts I was putting out, just by thinking them, were materialising without me doing anything physical to assist them. My thoughts were teaching me the power behind them. Was I thinking all of these events into a reality? I knew I was not looking for anything. I was very happy and content with my life. All of these events had happened to me, but what I thought about them was up to me. My thoughts were my own and I knew that I had a choice about whether to pay attention, or not, to what was happening. Boy, I was so wrong!

After these first sets of dreams/experiences, I was reading more and more books, trying to find a truth, a reason, behind it all. Many of the books helped but none of them could give me an explanation that I felt happy about, or could easily live with. Then I started noticing that I would say things that I did not feel I had personally thought. They even sounded different to me. What I was saying was wise and to the point and delivered differently from the way I would normally say something. Where was this coming from? It felt as if someone else was talking through my body. I thought to myself, now they have even taken over my thoughts, they have managed to replace mine with theirs. It occurred to me that this might be what being possessed was like. But it did not feel at all negative; in fact it was so positive it was saintly. When this was happening to me, I would be talking to my friends or family and I would say this is not me talking. No wonder they thought I had lost the plot. I would see the concern on their faces and I would have to tell them, hey! I'm fine. I don't think they believed me.

Was this a split personality?

No, I was fully aware of myself, and this was obviously a thought form from outside of my normal awareness. But these thoughts knew things that I knew I had never learnt. When I spoke to other people in this field, they told me that it was my guardian angel or my spirit guides, but I knew it wasn't. I was aware that it was not separate like another energy, although it was more outside of me than inside. There was a point somewhere in my body that this was connected to. But I still had a lot of learning to do. Who was going to teach me?

Chapter 29
Teachers

Each person is ready for a new level of awareness, at his or her own pace. As teachers we need to recognise this. In order to help another person on their journey, you have to be aware of where they are and who they are. Then you can assist them in discovering themselves bit by bit. To be the teacher can be invigorating and frustrating at the same time. Patience is one of the major requirements of a life teacher, or light worker, as we are known. As a teacher in this field you have knowledge and understanding on many levels. It may be clear to you what is going on, but this has to be comprehensible to the person sitting in front of you. You must be able to deliver information on the level that the student is on, just as normal schoolteachers do. You cannot talk about A-level subjects to a seven-year-old; they would think you were crazy.

I have tested this theory by giving people information connected to another level of their awareness, and it goes way beyond them. This is because they are working on a physical level, but I knew that on another level of their awareness what I said was understood. The result of this test was that a few months later this person became aware of that information, on their physical level (stepping down), and told me that it now made sense to them. I know that with this type of teaching we can deliver information from other levels, as long as we interpret this and let the student know that it will be understandable at a later date.

The type of teacher you are depends on the message you have to deliver, and the student who is receiving the message. In my field of intuitive work, I cover many different levels of awareness. I am only aware of which direction my teaching will go or what level of awareness I will use once a student is sitting in front of me.

We are all teachers, even though we may not as yet have woken up to our truth or uncovered our secret. Once we have, we will automatically need to share what we have discovered, because it is so incredibly amazing. We ourselves are permanently learning, even after we have woken up to our truth, because there are so many levels of knowing to discover. Try to remember to always work where you are in your own awareness and don't rush ahead of yourself. The reason I say this is because you will become aware of other levels but will not necessarily be able to step them down in a clear and understandable way. ALL IN GOOD TIME.

How to find a good teacher

Word of mouth is normally the best way to find a good teacher. But in this examination of life, anyone or anything can be your teacher, because we all learn from experience. This is called living. You will soon know if a teacher suits you. It swiftly becomes apparent. But as you grow, you may well outgrow your teacher. This is fine and you must move on. You may not ever need another teacher.

Most people come to me by word of mouth, and everyone I have assisted is still my pupil. This does not mean that they are slow or that I am no good as a teacher; quite the opposite. There are so many levels and levels within levels that the learning is never-ending.

As I grow and learn more, so do the people who come to see me. Some people I see on a regular basis and others only once a year. When you reach a new stage/level, it is nice to be able to share this with someone who knows where you are. Doing this with a teacher can help you understand it even more.

There isn't a book like the Yellow Pages that you can use to find this type of life teacher; there are not that many of us around. I find that during my everyday life I meet people and say a few words to them and they are amazed because it was just what they needed to hear at that moment. Children are some of the best teachers around because their thinking is so fresh and new. But the type of teacher we are discussing here is one who knows about the bigger picture.

The main thing that people need help with is getting to know their truth and, more importantly, maintaining it. Read books; go along to workshops. The person at the workshop might not be your teacher but someone there might know the teacher you are looking for. Please remember that thought creates, so voice the thought that you require a teacher.

Back to who was going to be my teacher. Who could help me make sense of it all and really put it in its right place? The only people who understood a lot of what was going on with me were mediums or clairvoyants. I contacted as many as I could find and each of them told me certain things that helped, but it was still not enough. I wanted to talk to an expert in this field that I had discovered. I went to the Arthur Finely College in Stanstead for a few days; this is an old family estate dedicated to the study of spirituality. It was while I was there that I discovered the names for the different abilities I had, as well as some I didn't know about. But nothing I found seemed to be what I was looking for. But I did decide I was not going to be a medium, despite the fact that I was good at it. I found that I was an incredible healer, and even a trance medium. But there was nothing that seemed to really encompass all that I knew.

It took me a while to realise that the person I was looking for to teach me was myself. In order for this to happen, I would need students to work on. I was fortunate to have a group of girlfriends, who presented me with many life situations and many different psychic events that they had experienced which they needed help with. Through my helping them, my wisdom seemed to come into its own. I had found my teacher, who was with me any time I wanted her; she was there and she was amazing. When it finally clicked, it all made so much sense. It was like a giant jigsaw puzzle that needed the final piece to reveal the whole picture, or one of those three-dimensional illustrations that you have to look at for quite a while before you can see the image that is hiding there.

Chapter 30
Existence

To understand the complexity of existence is almost impossible, and so most of the time we don't even try. It is so overwhelming that when we start trying to unravel its mysteries, we tend to end up following one direction and then getting lost, never reaching a conclusion.

I will try to explain existence, as I know it, in a pure and simple way. But it is a little complex, so you need to pay attention.

There is one thing (let's call it a cell, not that it is) which has the potential to be anything it so desires. When this cell subdivides itself into many more cells, each one of these can be what it wants to be, while still being the original cell. The cell becomes what it is going to be when thought enters the picture, so at this moment in time let's say that thought and cells are human beings, as well as a vast array of other things on other levels of existence. Remember, it is thought that creates. So thought created life on Earth and cells created what thought wanted. The cell is the condensed matter; thought is the energy that came from what we call God/all that is. When this cell is somewhere, it will become what and where it finds itself, and it will only change when it is in some other place or something has had an effect on it (a foreign body or virus).

To really understand existence on all levels, we would need to be part of each of these cells (which we have been and continue to be), because we are all part of the first original cell and the thought that created it. The reason we are generally unaware of this is because to be something that you are not, you have to forget who you are and, just like the cell, become where you are. It is the same as an actor playing a part in a movie and believing that it is real. Can you now see why I called this book *Our Secret Movie*?

Because we are playing the role of human being, our full attention is focused on that awareness. If you were to take your awareness and place it in another area, then your attention would be in two places of awareness at the same time. You have a contract to fulfil in your movie called Earth, but that does not mean that you cannot play a role in your spare time, in another place on a different level. You are then existing in two separate realties, at the same time. The part of us that is in another reality can perceive more about our true being than the part playing the movie on planet Earth. When we choose to be aware of the nature of our existence, and we free our mind to know more, this is enlightenment, which is to see, hear, sense and know more clearly.

When we perceive another level of existence, it is perceived through thought, which is part of our mind. All the cells in our body become aware and respond too. Every single cell in our body has all the information and all the abilities of all the other cells in existence. Each cell is a mini-universe, with the capability of becoming anything that exists.

If you were looking inside a body with a microscope, watching all of your cells being lots of different things, such as lungs, blood, heart, kidneys or fat cells, you would see each one of these cells going through living, dying and transforming themselves into new cells - a continual cycle until your body dies. Then what is left is the thought that created them in the first place. This thought is what we call life after death - this is what continues, remembering that thought is from the mind.

It is impossible to fully explain all of existence because you would have to be separate from it (all that is) to be able to see it in its entirety, looking from outside of it. And there is nothing that is not it (all that is).

So to explain the existence of Earth and its life forms, which a lot of people believe is all that exists, you would have to be on the outside of it. The astronauts who have travelled in space have seen existence from another place, and what do they see? Just one big bluish ball floating in space. They only know that it is more than that because they came from that world.

However, there is another way. It is possible to put our minds in another place that is not Earth as we know it, and in this awareness Earth life is something very different to what we know it to be. This is what a lot of my book is about - bringing that awareness into your everyday Earth life.

Then there is death, or no longer participating in the Earth movie, free from condensed matter (cells). The information that comes after clinical death is amazing and so very different from what we are aware of. It is always described as unconditional love, or as way beyond our wildest imagination. There are no words that can give it a description because words are not used. Words are symbols that are used only on Earth because of time and space. After Earth death there is no such thing as time and space.

Discovering existence was so mind-blowing. It was there all the time; I only had to choose to know it. How I did that was to let go, not try, just allow each stage of this journey I was on to unfold. There is a process that we go through, although it does vary slightly from person to person. I think about something that someone has asked me, then I let go and the answer appears within my mind. Sometimes it is hard to let go, and sometimes the answer has many different facets. It is our need for there to be only one simple explanation for the truth that interferes with our easily understanding the truth. As human beings, we want everything to be black or white, when in truth there is no such thing. There is nothing that truth can attach itself to because it is nothing which is the ultimate truth. And it is impossible to talk or describe nothing in its magnificence.

Chapter 31
Memory

As we go through life we gain many experiences, each of which has an effect on our being and which forms part of our character. So we build who we are as we grow through the natural cycles of life and the experiences that we have along the way. But at all times there is a core part of us that is more constant than the effects of experience. (It feels as if it is inside us but in truth it is everywhere.) This part is our essence, our truth, our soul and our spirit. We overshadow our true self with life's experiences and the body we live in.

When we are small children we walk and talk, being who we are and always expressing what we feel. As we grow older, we are taught to hide most of those ways and learn to fit in with our social groups. This is what is called living on memory, saying who and what we are by what we have already been. This suppresses our truth and keeps our secret hidden, not only from the world but also from ourselves. Then there comes a time when we question who we are, what we are here for, or even what we are doing. We start to look at ourselves and no longer know what our truth is. We are no longer that child who embraced life and did not hide. We cannot go back, only forward.

Each experience we have had on our journey has taught us how to be, and yet we do not feel as if we are being who we truly are. We perform for an audience; we play the role that society requires. The reason we do this is because we have a great need to be loved. So we do what we think we have to do in order to be loved. The way we live does work well for a short period of time. Then we reach a point when we question life and, unfortunately, something else comes along to distract us. When you look back at who you have become and discover how you became that person, and then decide to be who you truly are, this is the day when you start to be loved for who you are. You start by caring for yourself and getting to know yourself better, and then you discover a whole part of you that was missing. When you first discover it, you realise that you always knew it was there, just not exactly where or what it was.

Once I discovered my true self, it answered all the questions I'd had. It gave me a sense of peace and happiness, but I still had to learn how to live with this new person, whilst still being the old one I had always been. Accepting that it was all me was the greatest thing that I did for myself. By taking responsibility for all of these things that were happening to me, I was finally able to realise that they were there to teach me how to be more of myself, and in the process of doing so I could pass on this magical truth to others.

If we do not acknowledge these parts of ourselves, then we will always be only a part of what we could be and we will spend our lives searching for something to make us feel whole. To join these other aspects of myself together was hard for me to do, because there was an incredible magnificence about this bigger part that was too good for this body of mine and far too good for the planet we live on. It felt as if there was no place that was safe for it to exist here. Its beauty to me was far too perfect to be seen within the confines of a human body. It was like trying to fit a twenty-foot-tall, iridescent, sparkling, floating, beautiful presence into a normal-size average body that in no way could reflect its truth. I was scared. I felt that I could not do this beauty justice.

Chapter 32

Enlightenment

Everyone is looking for enlightenment at some point on his or her journey through life, and enlightenment is reached at different times for everyone. Well, I will let you in on a secret; everyone already has enlightenment, every human being on this planet has a light inside him or herself. The trick is to turn it on. Most of the time people will search everywhere but inside themselves in an attempt to find the switch and turn it on. To turn the switch on is not an accurate description, because the light is always on; you are always shining. It is more a case of knowing that you are enlightened and not looking for something that is already there. You need to start projecting that light, to feel it or become aware of it. There are many books, classes, lectures and retreats that can help you connect to your inner light. That is all they can do. It is your choice to become aware of your light or not. The first step is to choose it.

This is what I did. I chose to let this beauty shine through me, and then people started to notice it. They saw something in me that was so familiar that it made them feel good. What it was that they saw in me was what they knew existed within themselves. It was not on a conscious level that they were aware, but on a soul level. My being was assisting their being to become their truth. I was helping them to discover their secret. It was as if the light inside me had been dusted off and was able to shine and light the way for others as well.

Chapter 33
Helping

We all try to help our fellow beings in many ways. Sometimes, however, this help is detrimental to that person. When a person needs to learn a lesson and yet the people in their lives continually help them to resolve the issue, then they are unable to learn the lesson for themselves. What happens then is that the same situation will appear again in a different format. Because you solved it for them last time, they will rely on you to fix it again, which of course you will, if you can. But this makes the other person weak and you strong. You will always feel elevated by your position, which encourages you to continue helping. The more this process is repeated, the more you become involved in a vicious cycle, which will eventually become a drain on you. To break the cycle, you would appear to be unkind by not helping. But not to help in these circumstances would be a great gift of learning for the two of you. The other person would not see this until the lesson was learned, tested and finished with. When we learn something, we will always be tested to see if we understand what we have learned. This changes as we progress.

I am very rarely tested these days because I always look to see what I could learn from any event or situation. I'll give you an example of what I am talking about. A friend has run into financial difficulty and you help her/him out. Everything is fine for a period of time. Then this friend runs into further financial difficulty and again you help out. The friend will always run into financial difficulty one way or another until he/she learns to handle their finances and live within their earnings. This will only happen when financial help from you, or anyone else who might be helping, stops. This applies to all recurring problems. It is very important to know when to help and when not to. Helping hands can do more harm than good to both of you.

We grow because we learn by our mistakes or our successes. We never grow when we continually avoid or ignore problems. When something in your life is a problem, always look at it from many different angles, to see if there is something you can do to change, solve or learn from it. I know this is easy to say, but if you can train yourself to do this, you will be amazed at the difference it will make to your life and, of course, the lives of the people around you who offer help and assistance. People help because they care about and love you. But to have a greater understanding of helping and love would be a greater gift to you and the world.

Chapter 34

Love

Love is our connection to the world. Yes, love in its purity is what makes life special. Our need to be connected is where love starts. Love exists in our soul, and this level of our being does not know separation in the way that we do. On a physical level, we see ourselves as individual and disconnected from the whole (all that is). Love has many avenues by which to show itself - mother love, child love, animal love, love of life, partner love - but in all of this love is a connection to someone or something outside of ourselves. The love that feeds the soul is the love from our essence, that exists from within the soul and creates the soul, which originates from "all that is". This love is our true connection to all that is. Once we have found this pure love, we find our connection to our higher selves, which is part of all that is. This is the truest, most unconditional love of all.

We are oblivious to our truth by design. Throughout our lives we have been taught to put others before ourselves. To find the love within us we need to love ourselves, and this is often regarded as selfish or grandiose. This was so in the past, but today it is a different story.

The way to love ourselves is not to do so in a selfish way, thinking that we are more important or better than any other human being. It is by learning to know who we truly are. This is achieved by understanding what makes us happy, what we have, what we feel and what we really think. This means not doing what we have been taught or brought up to believe in, but to reassess it all and see what we come up with now.

The path of self-investigation is an immense journey of discovery, sometimes very scary, often unbelievably surprising. It is through this journey that we start to find ourselves and our own unique connection to unconditional love (all that is). This love has no boundaries and is everlasting; once it is known it will always be there. Love on a physical level will always grow and change and can even melt away. Love on a soul level, however, is solid, constant and more real than any reality we know of on Earth. The feeling that we experience with a partner when we fall in love is very close to unconditional love. But as time goes by, in any relationship, everyday life and experiences enter the equation and cloud the true essence of love. The love that we found with this partner was our own love, because we can only truly feel our own essence, which is (all that is). This means that when a being outside of you helps you to discover your love, you also discover their love. Remember, there is nothing other than love and this love is light. This love is energy, and this love is creation.

When we fall deeply in love, we feel there is no separation. We feel as one. This place is so wonderful that it is scary. As we progress, we feel as if we have dissolved and, at this point, fear enters the equation and causes us to protect ourselves because we are vulnerable and exposed. We feel that we might disappear if we don't hold on to our own identity, and yet being one with our partner was so beautiful and real at the beginning.

It is this process that we go through that causes us all the problems in our relationships. When fear rears its ugly head it can make us feel jealous or weak. It can make us withdraw, create anger or confuse us and make us frustrated. As time goes by, if a relationship stands the test of time, we allow ourselves to try again. We drop the fear that caused us to forget our love, and hey presto! There it is. This is when we learn to embrace love - not hide or run from it.

The reason we fall in love is because we see the essence of the being we fall in love with. What is on the outside of that person when love is in the equation is not important, because the soul shines through. Don't forget that the other people see your soul too. Because you love, you are shining. When fear enters the picture, it forms a shadow over the soul/essence. Then all we see is the ego self. This is the personality that has been formed from life experiences. (The ego self is not a bad thing but sometimes it thinks it is the truth and the only truth. This ego self has a role to play. Only when it tries to be what it is not does it cause us problems.) If the person's personality is not true to its soul essence, it affects the relationship and can be almost impossible to live with.

You may have heard people say, 'I love him/her, but I don't like him/her.' This is what is happening at that moment in their connection. A relationship where the people involved are not connected to their essence can still have moments of connection, such as a romantic evening or an intimate conversation in which they are able see each other's essence. After these moments all is well, but the connection cannot last for long periods of time. This is because they jump back into their ego self, which is full of fear and protective instincts. If a person lives their life close to its true nature, then when fear enters it does not have such a drastic effect on their being. This is because the difference between the ego self and the soul essence is very small. This, in my opinion, is what makes a good relationship of any kind - walking, talking and living your truth. This connection to your truth helps you to shine through all of life's connections, not just loving partnerships. This is all about being happy with yourself and being able to withstand all of life's ups and downs. Happiness lies within the context of being, not doing. So when you learn how to just be, you learn the secret of happiness, and that happiness is reflected in everything you do.

Unconditional love

Unconditional love is hard to describe because it is not attached to any particular thing or person, but I will do my best to tell you what it is.

In truth, it is you; it is what you are made of, although you are not made (created). In your truth, you just are. Have I lost you yet? 'Unconditional' means that there is no reason or requirement, no attachment at all, no form or structure.

Love, as we know it to be, has many meanings, which in contrast are all based on attachment and requirement. So when we hear these two words together - unconditional love - they don't make sense, they wipe each other out. This is because on a physical level it is impossible to really understand; it belongs to another part of your being, to what we call your essence/soul. The only way to know this is to know your essence. I am not saying that when you discover your essence/soul you will discover unconditional love. I am saying that your essence is unconditional love; so to describe it you would be describing your soul/ essence. This is the tricky part, how to describe the indescribable. It is (although it is not anything that can be called an it, for it does not have any boundaries, so there is no end or nowhere where it is not).

I said that to describe the essence/soul is impossible, but here I go again. Now you know that it has no defined structure, but it does have a form of content that is present and living and flowing freely within everything, and also outside of everything that has any type of boundary.

You cannot picture the soul or understand it; you can only know it. Then it is no longer an it; it is everything, and, being pure potential, it becomes whatever is required.

When this pure potential/essence/soul/unconditional love becomes a human being, it is still pure potential at the same moment, in what we call time. It is forever changing, yet always remaining constant at the same moment. So as a human being we are unconditional love, only we are not being it because we are within a reality that is a design, so we know ourselves as a separate identity. So to truly understand what I am trying to describe, you would have to connect to your truth. I am sorry, but this is the only way, other than by dying, that you will know your essence.

There is nothing more rewarding on this planet than to witness another person connect to their essence and experience unconditional love. They do not realise that they are experiencing their truth at this moment, but the more they encounter this love, the more they learn and the more they grow, and one day they are able to accept that this most beautiful love is them. This is the start of the journey of bringing that love into every moment of their lives.

Chapter 35

Wanting

Have you ever noticed the amount of pleasure we receive from wanting? Perhaps we want a car, a lover, a house, a new job or our connection to life. We gain the greatest amount of pleasure thinking about ourselves living this wanting. Seeing ourselves in the new car, kissing the lover or being connected to our essence. When we receive what we want we are overcome and really happy because we have already experienced our wants in our mind. It feels familiar. This wanting and receiving is never quite enough. Don't get me wrong. It is very fulfilling and exhilarating, but it does not fill the gap. So before long, we are on to our next wanting. This pattern continues throughout life, and the only thing that fills that gap is connecting to your essence. When you receive this want, it is so powerful that it is too good to be true, and it never stops feeling that way. The only thing that can happen is that you forget to feel it. And this happens because we get caught up in life's dramas and forget the bigger picture. At this point you realise that all the wanting that you have ever had is attached to this. Being in your essence this does not mean that you will never again want anything on a physical level. This wanting will turn into 'That would be nice but it's OK if I don't have it, for I don't need it to make me happy and complete'.

Please remember that thought is the creative power that lies behind your life, and by wanting, you are putting that thought out there. It is action that gives that thought a reality. So if you want, go out and get.

Sometimes, we think we want things to make us happy, only to discover that when we have them, they do not do what we thought they would. This is the hardest disappointment that we could experience, because we put so much into want fulfilment being the answer to our lives. When you truly know yourself, the wanting changes. You know that whatever you want can never give you what you already have, and it is only ever going to be extra pleasure. So if it does not happen, it is not such a great disappointment.

I used to say, 'All I want is … (whatever that want was at the time)'. Once I got what I wanted, I would really enjoy it for a period of time, then I would move on to the next 'all I want is …' and this would appear. Then one day my husband said to me, 'You are never satisfied, you always want more.' I thought about this and realised that what I was saying was that if I have this then I have it all. Today, this has changed to 'I would like this'. I now know that there is nothing out there that could ever give me all that I want, because I know that I have it all by simply being me. If tomorrow everything that I know and love in my life disappears, I still have it all. I have me. This is not acceptable or understandable unless you are living your truth. This is how people who lose everything continue to live and even have a smile on their face. It is not easy but it is possible. And I think the subject of the next chapter plays the main part in our living our truth.

Chapter 36
Attitude

Attitude is the way we chose to respond to what we see, hear, taste and feel. It is a response to our five senses, as well as conditioning from our experience and our upbringing. How many times have you heard statements like 'You need to change your attitude' and 'He has the wrong attitude'? To change your attitude, you need to change the way you see the world. When we adopt a stubborn attitude, we are refusing to view the situation or person in a different light. We are being rigid and self-protective. We are refusing to change.

So attitude is all about seeing and being where you want to be. This is fine, until you reach a point when you feel as if everything is going against you, when it seems that all you face is confrontation with everyone around you. OK, so what is it that could possibly change our attitude?

Yes, it has to be something quite big that shakes us to our bones. This shake-up call happens out of the blue. It can appear in many different guises, but what happens is what is important. That is that you become lost in a moment of no time, you are free to be. It is this moment that changes your attitude. If it doesn't, then there will be other shake-up calls along the way. If you choose not to take advantage of these calls, then you will always feel as if there is something missing from your life.

What I am saying is that we need to free ourselves from our attitude; not be set in our ways. You need to adapt your attitude until you are free to respond. This then turns your fixed attitude into an adaptable, flexible attitude.

If I have the attitude that I am not worthy, then I will not be worthy.

If I have the attitude that everything happens for a reason, then it will.

If I chose to feel, see, hear, taste and sense, I will not have an attitude; I will have the ability to be me.

My attitude was almost at the point of disappearing because of everything that was happening to me. I could not hold on to one way of thinking and I found it really hard to take a stance on anything. It was a very confusing time for me. I could not say who I was; there was nothing I could attach myself to. I realised that I did not need to be one thing or another; my labels were disappearing one by one, and although it was scary, it was freeing me from the concept of the me whom I'd always known. This new-found freedom was allowing me to change, but not into anything in particular, more into nothing. And yet this nothing felt more real than any attachment or attitude I'd ever had about life. It reminded me of an aura picture of myself that was taken at Arthur Finley College. This picture was amazing. When the lady who took the picture spoke to me about it, she thought that I had just been meditating. She told me that the colours represented a connection to the higher energy fields. She was able to tell me many interesting things about myself and my life through this picture. I didn't realise it at the time but this photograph was to have a major effect on many different people. In the picture I was in the middle of this amazing golden glow with a white light running through me. There was a red glow around the middle of my body and a beautiful green glow around my right hand. I could barely see myself in the picture.

When I had returned home, I popped round to see my mother and showed her the picture. As she looked at it, I told her what all the different colours were meant to represent. All of a sudden she jumped back and shook her head. I asked her what was wrong and she said, 'That was really weird. I have just seen my mom looking back at me from your picture.' I took the picture from her and looked at it, then all of a sudden I could see my nan, then it changed and I saw my Auntie Eileen!

I handed it back to mom and she saw the same faces. She then saw other relatives who had been dead for years. It just kept morphing; she was seeing men, women and children from different cultures. She sat transfixed by this picture; tears were streaming down her face and she said that she just could not believe what she was seeing.

I showed the picture to other people and the same thing happened again. They all saw what Mom had. Even when I showed it to people who were not related to me, they could see their family members in the picture. This was really freaky. What was happening? Was it the power of suggestion? I tested it out by giving the picture to others and not saying anything other than telling them to look at it. Yet again, the same thing happened. This was not the case with other aura photographs that I had looked at.

On my grandmother's ninety-third birthday, we went to the nursing home to celebrate with her. She'd had visitors all day, people coming and going. When I arrived my uncle and auntie were there, as well as my mom and Yvette. I happened to mention to my auntie that nan's face and hers had appeared in my picture. We started talking about the picture, which led on to us talking about other different energies. My uncle said that when he had gone for his heart check-up the nurse had told him that there was a lot of energy in his hands. He moved his hand in my direction so that I could feel it, which I did. I put my hand about ten inches above his and asked if he could feel my energy. 'Wow, that's so powerful!' My auntie wanted to feel it, but the room was small and nan was sitting in the middle, in her chair. I moved so that she could feel my energy. She put her hand out and I placed my hand over hers. I was not prepared for what happened next. Neither was anyone else. My auntie cried out, 'Ohh, ohhh, ohhhh!' Mom stood up and held her other hand, which she had reached out for help. I looked into her eyes and saw such sorrow and pain. She started crying and saying, 'I am so scared, what's happening to me? What's going on?' We reassured her and told her that it was OK and to just let it out, which she did. All the hurt in her life that she had never really dealt with; the loss of her baby brother, the great loss of her younger sister, who died of breast cancer at the age of twenty-seven and left four young children behind. All of this emotion surfaced, before she experienced the most amazing relief. I still had my hand on hers. I was still giving her energy when I looked over at my nan, who said to me in a matter-of-fact way, 'Don't give her too much!' I smiled and said I wouldn't. It was as if nan really knew what was going on. The strange thing was that I always knew that she was aware of more than most people are, only she never had the need to talk about it. It was as if a part of her, the higher part, was always communicating with me, but her physical self was not aware of this. My auntie told me afterwards that she had this incredible overwhelming feeling of unconditional love. It was so strong and so peaceful and so, so special. This energy had a major effect on her life and her family's life, which at the time were troubled. This experience changed my auntie's attitude to life, which in turn changed her life.

Chapter 37
Mind, Body, Soul

There are three major parts to the human being:
Mind. The intellect and reason
Body. Sensory awareness and action
Soul. Multi-dimensional awareness, connection to all that is.
Most people on planet Earth acknowledge only the body and
the mind. At this time in the evolutionary phase of existence, we are
becoming more aware of the soul. It is our responsibility to evolve into
the new phase of being. This process has been going on for thousands
of years; it is nothing new. It is now the time to evolve further and put
it into practice. The mind and the body are part of the soul. The soul
houses your spirit, which comes from your essence. Your essence is your
truth in a particular format. The complete truth is all that is and all
that is not. The place where soul/essence is known is of another reality,
very different to the mind/body reality. What mind and body do is allot
descriptions and symbols to the experience of soul. The descriptions that
are received about your soul are never translatable through our normal
understanding. They are beyond physical and mental description.

We all have moments in our lives in which we have experienced an
aspect of soul, such as falling in love, giving birth, orgasm, death and
great pain. Within these moments there is an openness to our soul that
gives us the opportunity to discover aspects of essence - a moment when
connection is right there, within you. And the only way to continue this
connection is to let go and experience it. We are afraid of this power
that is in us and we try to control it, contain it or run from it, when all
we really need to do is let go and then embrace it.

There are many moments throughout our journey when we are able
to connect to our essence. Each of these moments is a reminder of us.
The reason it is easier to connect at moments of extreme emotion is that
we are at the point of letting go and this is an opening in our being to

our higher selves. Mind, body, soul; each has its own unique awareness, and by being fully present in mind, you can connect to a part of essence. By being fully in body, you can connect to a part of essence. But if you are fully in soul, there is no Earthly mind or body - it is just an illusion that, as an essence, you created to experience what you are not.

There are different layers of awareness of essence, and this is down to how you got there (by death, astral travelling, meditation or enlightenment) and where in there you are (dependent on your contract). Within each layer of reality there are many truths (reality being who you think you are, which will define what you are, which all depends on where you find yourself), just as there are many parts to the body and many experiences that you can have. There are many layers to the mind and there are many different minds, all connected to the part of the reality they are in. For example, the human being has a mind that is bigger and more knowing than it; the soul has a mind that is more knowing than its awareness; the spirit has a mind … and so on, until there is only mind of essence left. After this there is nothing or, more to the point, no thing, which has no need and, therefore, has no mind to know. The Earthly mind and body come to a point where there is no more (death). The mind and the body have a start and an end. The soul and its mind have an end. The spirit and its mind have an end. The essence has an end. The all that is has it all. But the 'nothing' is the truth, and there is nothing there to mind.

The essence is infinite and is a continuous flow, which would appear to be growing. Each growth has new perspectives and new truths. You will only see the truth within the level of awareness that you are in. So as we grow in our essence, the picture grows and changes too. This does not mean that what came before was not true; it is true in that level of awareness. When a baby learns to walk it is the greatest thing. When that baby learns to run it is the greatest thing, but it does not wipe out the walking.

When we learn the alphabet and then learn to read, the advancement does not wipe out the first learning but just improves it. Our essence is present in us and at all times, for our essence is who we truly are, as long as we are being. If it were not there, then we would not be even a soul or a spirit. Our mind and body are a way of representing our essence in an Earthly reality, created so we can experience separation, for this is something that we are not able to do in our essence, which comes from all that is.

It is impossible to understand this "all that is", and trying to explain it in any way gives it definition. The truth (all that is) is itself, not a self, with no substance, no requirement, nothing to know, but all that could be and has been and none of it. But the 'nothing' before and after the 'all that is' is the truth. Only there is nothing other than to know it is the truth.

Chapter 38
Title

The reason I chose *Our Secret Movie* as the title of this book is that our lives are very much like a movie, in more than one way. When we watch a TV screen or a cinema screen, the movies seem so real that they can make us cry; yet we remain aware that it is just a film. When we watch a movie, what we are really watching is lots of still pictures flashing on and off in a fraction of a second. There are as many blank, black spaces as there are frames, yet we see it as a continuous moving picture. This is the same as our lives. The vibration picture we know as life is made up of frames and blank, black spaces. Everything that we know, even ourselves, is in truth a continuous flashing on and off of pictures frames. We are, in fact, on/not on, in/not in or there/not there. This is different from on and off, as we believe the opposite of on is off, when in fact they are two different things, so the opposite of on is not on.

With each new flash of picture, we and all around us become a new reality. The speed at which this happens is inconceivable because it is faster than the speed of light. When this process is viewed from a soul level, it appears that everything is standing still, and we know it not to exist in a moving format. We see a picture appearing then disappearing. The picture that appears is opaque.

If you were to stare at a person for a long time, not thinking (I know that's hard), the face starts to change. If you can manage to still keep staring, all kinds of faces will appear, including animals and ugly, scary faces. If you can keep staring after this stage, the light around the person changes and the face disappears and you are in the space in between the picture. This space is very close to how our souls perceive existence. I must say that the space I am referring to as blank, black space is more colourful to our soul than the most iridescent of colours.

So when we are viewed by the soul, we are seen in the same way that we watch a TV screen, real enough to make us cry, but not real enough to believe that it is the truth. So next time when you sit down to watch TV think about how you are affected by what you are watching.

The effect that my aura picture was having on people who looked at it started to happen when I was working with clients. My face was doing exactly what my aura picture did. I would be sitting, talking, and I would become aware of my energy changing. All of a sudden whoever I was with would be transported to a different level of awareness. They would see all these incredible faces that were somehow familiar, but not known to them in a physical way. It would really scare them the first time and they would jump and blink a lot to find their composure. I would encourage them to let go and just see where it went. Most of the time it would end by showing them a face that they really knew. This person could be dead or alive. It was as if the energy of the person that they saw was being superimposed on to me.

The first time this happened to me was at the Arthur Finley College. We were in a large room, waiting to see a medium do a trance presentation. I had not experienced this before and did not know what to expect. It was quite a bizarre thing to watch. Although I was having a hard time believing that the person doing the demonstration was for real, I could sense energy all around her and could see changes. The lady who sat next to me asked if I believed all this and I told her what I felt. The next day this lady and I were roped into posing for the photographs for a new brochure. At one point we were asked to stand next to the gate and look as if we were talking, which we did. We started talking about the night before and how we had found what happened hard to believe it. The lady told me that she had lost her son five years earlier. All of a sudden, I felt a very powerful surge of energy sweep over me, which did not go away. The lady was crying and I hugged her. Out of my mouth came the words 'I am OK, Mom'. The lady cried from the bottom of her heart. I held her tight. I felt as if there was someone else with me; I was still there but this energy was stronger than mine. It was so overwhelming. I knew it was her son. I did not have to say anything. The lady looked at me; she knew without doubt that she had just been hugged and spoken to by her dead son. This was so weird. We both knew that it was there to show us that trance mediumship can and does happen, even if we're sceptical. But the most important thing for her was that she was able to know that her son was OK and she was able to hold him one more time.

This lady went away happy and free to move on. I went away feeling very strange and quite scared about the fact that something could use my body in this way. It has happened to me many times since that day, only it does not bother me any more. It gives people what they need: proof and experience of life after death.

How I understand this process now is very different from then, when I was raw and inexperienced in this new-found ability. To understand what truly happens would only make sense on other levels of awareness. There is only one, and because we are all part of the whole, I could be any part of that whole in any time frame, because it was all in the same space, because the truth is there is no space and there is no time. It did take me a long time to reach this point, but when I did it I realised that it was all so simple, I only had to accept it, which allowed me to know it in its truth.

Chapter 39

Writing My Book

When I write a part of my book, I feel a great sense of relief and accomplishment. This tells me that I am supposed to do this. Just before I write, I am aware of a strange feeling that engulfs me and I feel as if I am supposed to be doing something. It is only when I sit down and write a passage that I feel good and free to get on with my everyday life. It took me a long time to figure this out. I found that I felt lethargic and could not bring myself to do housework, to do anything in fact, until I had contributed to this book. There has never been a moment when I have sat down and said to myself, I must write. Everything I have written has happened on the spur of the moment. Thoughts just drop into my head, then I put pen to paper. I know that I have a deadline and it is going to take me eighteen months to complete. I began writing in February 2001, so it will be finished by August 2002. This deadline and timing are from my essence. I know it will be finished on time.

It is now 21 February 2004 and, yes, I am still writing this book! I did complete it on time, but I was still going through the editing process. I let family and friends read it, and they all said it needed more of my magic and my experiences, which is what I am adding at this precise moment. Why am I telling you this? Well, the medium that I went to see for my fortieth birthday present from Julie told me that this book will be out there two years after it should have been. She asked me if I understood what she meant and I said yes, even though I didn't. Now, at this moment, I do understand. It will be two years in August since I finished the book, exactly two years after I thought it would be out there in the marketplace.

Chapter 40
Process

To be who we truly are, we need to really get to know who we are. But finding out who we are is where most people have trouble. The reason is that we pay too much attention to one aspect of ourselves and are unable to let go of our idea of ourselves soon enough. We must move on. We have to almost rediscover our body and mind and learn to connect to our soul. To do this we need to separate each part and rediscover each part on its own merits. I know that this might seem laborious, but believe me, it brings the greatest reward that there is on this planet: the secret that is the truth of you.

Once we have discovered each part, we need to link it all back together. We can fail quite easily at this point, because when we pay too much attention to one aspect of our being we become unbalanced.

Sense and logic are two very separate parts of our being, and each is a necessity for normal bodily functioning. Everything we do is at all times being done with the full awareness of our soul, because we cannot exist without it. We tend to believe that connection to our soul or essence is something that we can achieve, by attending meditation classes, for example. But in actual fact, we have already got that connection. We are all soul/essence, experiencing being a human, not the other way round. So if we are our soul, why are we doing so much to try to be something that we are already? The reason is that we have become so caught up in the illusion of being human that that is all we see or know ourselves to be. Please remember that this is all by design (our contract).

So we need to start with the brain and the body and unravel them and put them back together, allowing them to function the way they are designed to. Everything in life and existence has a place and a function; problems occur when they are not doing what they are designed to do. The body has many functions. It is a tool, full of many sensory perceptors. It can do and discover all kinds of things but it cannot think!

That is the job of the brain, our computer. This is designed to teach us and to assist the body to take care of and protect itself. It is our organizer and our problem solver, and it can also discover the nature of things. Both of these are part of our soul as long as we are living. But our soul is still there, after our body and brain are dead and gone. So the soul is our truth, and the brain and body are there for the soul to exist in another way of being. The soul is how we connect to our wisdom and unconditional love (bliss).

We cannot get to our soul through our brain or our body so here is the tricky bit. We need to be fully present in our mind to allow our brain and body to access our soul/essence. In other words, we need to discover ourselves first on a physical level and then on a mental level in order to go beyond who we are and discover our mind, then do and live what we know ourselves to really be. This is when we are connected to our soul. This does not always apply, as in my case. But if you manage to work on your physical/mental aspects before you start the journey of discovery to your essence, it will be easier.

In my case, I had to work out life and beyond at the same time. It was very hard work, but the knowledge I gained through this was so vast that I would do it all over again.

Each part of our being needs to be what it is. You might think that it can't be anything else! You would be right up to a point. If Joe next door can do the splits easily, he is designed to be able to do so. This does not mean that you can or that you were meant to. So, it is your responsibly to your body and mind to discover what they are capable of and why. We all have a responsibility to become aware of the true nature of ourselves, to make the world we live in a better, easier place to be. Once you start to discover more and more of your truth, your life will make sense and form patterns that can help you to figure out what else you are here in this body, on this planet, living your life for.

Chapter 41

Growing on the journey

The pleasure of life is in the searching, in the journey, but we only tend to discover it when looking back. So, stop reading and look back and see just how far you have come, and please remember that the pleasure was there all the time. You were simply unable to see this truth because you did not know what lay ahead of you, if it was safe or whether or not you were taking the right path. This is fear where fear is not required. When you are there in your future event looking back, you discover that everything that happened was there for one reason or another, and that everything, good or bad, played a part in where you are now. By looking back you may discover that if you had just paid attention to a particular event at that time, you could have saved yourself a lot of heartache. You got there in the end. This means that you will learn what you came to learn, one way or another, and it is your free will that allows you to choose either the easy way or the hard way. And if you need to learn something the hard way for quicker growth, you will. We grow on all levels by learning and not standing still. It is always better to take action in a specific direction. This is the quickest way to know if something is right for you or not. The way we learn is either by the action working or not.

Then there is always sound advice. Now, we either take it in and listen, or we choose not to. The choice is ours. We act on it or we don't, but we will learn from it. Why make life a battle when it does not need to be? I guess what I am saying here is to always be sure to enjoy the searching and the journey. This way, when looking back, you have double the amount of pleasure in living. The pleasure I experience in my moments, hours, days, weeks is most of the time overwhelming. Looking back at the way my journey has played out so far feels indescribably satisfying. This is never easy and takes a lot of practice, but it sure is worth it.

Chapter 42
The light, bright side

'Always look on the light side of life, de dum, de dum, de dum, de dum, de dum ...' Even singing this song from the film *The Life of Brian* by Monty Python puts a big smile on my face and in my heart. There is always a light or bright side to life. Yes, even in our darkest moments. They are there to help us through and lift our spirits. It is not being naive to look on the light, bright side; it is a technique that we use to lighten a situation and help us to move on and let go.

How many times have you been to a funeral and heard people referring to funny events that happened to the person who has died, whereupon everyone laughs? How many times in the midst of crying have you laughed at yourself for being so silly?

In despair, there is always a moment of light. Be open enough to yourself to sense it and this will carry you through. The old saying 'Time heals all' is only true insofar as time allows us to distance ourselves from an event. Within this time, we are able to see more light and in light there sits truth. Time also allows us to look back and see a much bigger picture.

Laughter is contagious. It is also a release mechanism that allows us to have a moment of freedom from all of our everyday problems. And in that moment we are connected to our essence. To be able to see the funny, light or brighter side of life is a great gift that we all have. We have all been there in those serious moments when life is difficult and then someone laughs. Why is it that we apologize or feel guilty? What has happened is a natural response, in the same way that crying is. In fact, we should be apologizing for being too serious. There is really very little difference between all of our emotions - some are a negative response and some are positive. Even a negative emotional response in the right context can be great. They are all releasing stored energy and in doing so they have a cleansing effect on the body.

Sometimes, I forget to feel the lighter side of life because I spend most of my time with people who are going through emotional upset, and it can so easily rub off. This is why I need a great deal of empathy, rather than sympathy. If I sympathize, I lose myself in their situation. By empathizing, which is understanding, I am freer to see more clearly, which enables me to help. I teach people to step away from their problem and look at it through my eyes or the eyes of another. By observing, we automatically see more and also gain a sense of freedom from our situation.

Chapter 43
Boredom

This chapter came about because of my teenage son, whose two main phrases for a time were 'I'm hungry' and 'I'm bored'. Oh, by the way, this stage does eventually pass for all you parents out there with teenagers.

Boredom. What is it? I am always hearing people complaining that they are bored. What they really mean is they cannot find anything to do that will make them happy. There is always something to do; not wanting to do it is what creates the boredom. Normally, when you are bored, it is because you are comparing the moment you are in to a future or past event, and you feel that you would be happier if you were there. What you need to remember is that happiness is always with you, sitting on your shoulder; it is an attitude. There is only one way to get rid of boredom and that is to be present in each moment and live it, rather than waste it by looking back or forward to other moments of your life. Remember that each moment leads to the next and the future cannot happen without going through the now. In the now moment there is so much to learn - once you learn how to be in the now, that is. It has been a long time since I have felt bored, and I believe that boredom used to simply lead me to take action in one direction or another.

So boredom can be healthy - as long as you use it to take action. When you just sit there and moan, then it is decidedly unhealthy. I know that once we start to discover our true nature, boredom changes more into frustration. This happens because we are impatient, which is what created the boredom in the first place. To learn patience we need to be present in the moment. Yes, I know that I am repeating myself. But when I was working with my friend's son, and he told me that I had said something before, my reply to him was that for it to really sink in we need to hear something quite a few times. So, let go of boredom, let go of frustration, let go of past and future and live in the now and so discover patience, happiness and the secret of you.

I remember the way I used to live my life. It was always in a future event. I thought that my complete happiness lay within certain situations and places that had not yet come to fruition, such as the right house, having children or even just the right curtains to create the right room for my perfect life. I could not wait for my life to begin, but it was always in the future, just out of reach. It was not that I was not enjoying myself, or not enjoying where I was at that moment, but this perfect time was hidden within me, waiting for me to acknowledge it. The day I turned thirty-seven was the day I chose to be right where I was and to discover that I had been living my perfect life all along. I still look forward and plan for things in my future, but most of the time I am one hundred per cent in my now, and I never have enough time to enjoy all the things that are there for me in each moment. Boredom, what's that?

Chapter 44
Knowing

All that I now know (knowing meaning soul/spirit/essence knowledge) is to be shared with anyone that I meet on my journey through life. If I do not share my knowing, then the only being who benefits from it is me. When referring to me, this is I, the being, Sonya, who I know myself to be. You only know the I that is you. Everything that you know is yours, it belongs to you, because it is your knowing that is aware of it. I know that what I am telling you belongs to me, but when you know what I am telling you, and know it for yourself, then it becomes yours. So what I am sharing with the world is mine only until you know it, then it is ours. So if what I know is ours, there is no reason why I should not share this information. This sounds confusing, even to me, so I will provide you with an example.

I have discovered how to connect to my soul and I have found ways that can assist other people to discover this too. When I tell you what I have discovered, it is my discovery that I am telling you about. When I tell you how to discover this for yourself, it is still my technique that you are using to discover it with. When you use my technique it is still mine. But when you discover something more than you thought there to be in life, namely your soul, then this becomes your truth.

Here we go, hang on in there. Once you have found your soul, you will then know that there is only one real true thing. The energy essence that is the soul is the same energy essence that is you and I, and every other being that exists. To repeat myself, what I know belongs to all of us. This is why I share it.

Chapter 45

Perceiving

We perceive something on a physical level with our sensory body. That sensed information is delivered to the brain, and is then converted into information that we can understand. The brain categorizes each item of information it receives and stores it in our memory bank for future reference. This is a natural physical process, which is reinforced by teaching and life experience. During this process of teaching and experiencing we do not activate our sixth sense. We ignore it as much as we can because we are not helped to use it.

Our sixth sense is our natural Earth guide and is designed to help us to do the right thing (assist us with our contract). In the past, we used it in a small way to assist us in our journey of life. Then, when the human race went against its natural way of being and became more involved with its human aspect, it relied less on it. People who still used their ability were persecuted. People in a position of power were afraid of the wisdom that certain individuals were able to access. So laws were passed to stop anyone using this ability, and those found guilty of practising it were sentenced to death. Despite this, the people who enforced the laws - the landowners, or should we say the land conquerors - employed soothsayers or seers to make them more powerful. Even though it was against the law, people experienced their sixth sense.

When the Witchcraft Act was abolished, it made a big difference to the human race and our freedom to be. If it had not been, then I would not be writing this book for you. What is needed now is encouragement and teaching in the use of our natural sixth sense. We have all used it at one point or another in our life, although we may pass it off as something else. Religion and science have played a large part in our suppressing our sixth sense, although both have contributed to our world in other ways. Life is made up of many parts and it is now time to link all of these together, which will allow us to see the bigger picture. This planet now needs teachers to show us how to use all of our senses and connect to our essence. This is the next evolutionary stage of planet Earth.

Chapter 46

Change

Life is not static and can never be that way. Therefore, what we learn and comprehend today will be added to tomorrow, to advance it or to replace it. When we make a statement that implies that this is it and all it can be, this is when we fall short. For in every moment there is something new, and the more that is new, the more potential for change there is. By the time I have finished writing this book most of what I have told you could have changed slightly, and these changes will have a cause and an effect. There are things that stay static for longer because they are useful within an extended time frame. This does not of course mean that they have not changed or that they will never change. We need to free ourselves and our thoughts to allow change. This encourages us to grow. As for this book, when I have finished, I will read it and add the changes if they happen. But once it has gone to press, then what I have written applies to that moment in time. I may well need to produce a revised edition in the light of subsequent change.

Chapter 47
Cause and Effect

Cause and effect. We have all heard this phrase and I believe that we all accept it. But do we take on board what it really means? I don't think so. Everything that exists has a cause and and effect, and the only way this can happen is if there is only one event. For us to understand that, we have to realize that anything we don't do also has a cause and and effect on something. There is only one conclusion we can reach by accepting cause and effect, which is that there is no such thing as true space. We, and everything that exists, are joined together. This may not be visible but it is definitely the case. It is only space that allows us to know ourselves as separate, or should I say space and time, because according to the laws of time there is past, present and future. So if we accept that everything is one, for anything to have an effect on anything else, then everything exists all at the same moment (in time which is not real). There is nothing that is not connected. So everything that exists already exists within that moment (in time, which is not real). It is our natural human way of knowing that will not allow us to truly understand the time/space problem.

Once you have experienced your essence, then it all makes sense. It is so clear that you cannot understand why as human beings we find this so hard to comprehend. The reason is that in your essence you know yourself as everything and nothing. You know there is only one, but it is not one, as we know one to be, for there is no place where it is or where it is not. And for there to be one, it has to be confined to the one space. I hope you are managing to stay with me here. Okay, when we say one, we see it as a separate whole, where one in the sense of essence is all, with no end and no beginning. It just is and can only and always be one without definition. So by saying one, we are defining it. Even calling it an 'it' is giving it a definition. I am sorry, I wish that I could explain the unexplainable better. So the magical secret truth of us all is 'nothing', but this 'nothing' is everything and nothing that everything came from.

Chapter 48
Personal Belief

Have you ever wondered why it is that all the good mediums, gurus, avatars or anyone who has insight into life have so many people wanting to see them? And yet all the churches or other places of worship don't have people queuing up to the same extent. I believe that people today need more proof, and this proof has to be on a personal level. Everyone has the ability to find this personal level of knowledge. People today need to know that there is a reason to existence, and that there is more to us than the physical being we know ourselves as, and also that there is some form of life after death. This information can be delivered in many ways, but there is only one way that it can be known. That way is on a personal level, and then the knowing is yours. The only thing that others can do is to assist you with your discovery of your true self - whether the person assisting you is a priest, monk, teacher or rabbi; that is your choice. The important thing is your own personal discovery.

I did not have a person assisting me in my discovery, which made it a little harder on a physical level. I am not attached to any particular belief; only my own truth. Through this discovery I feel a part of all of life and its religions and philosophies and structures. By discovering my true nature, I discovered that everything that exists, exists inside of me. At the same time, I found myself to exist in everything outside of me. I don't think there could be a bigger contradiction than this.

Once we can understand that we are everything and yet we are nothing, we are left with: where am I? The answer is that we are nowhere and everywhere at the same time! So we cannot be defined. Only on a physical level do we see and know ourselves to have definition, but our essence is indefinable. And it is only an aspect of essence that is defined as a separate human being. There are other levels of awareness where we know ourselves to be a part of a whole. But the fact that we know ourselves means that we have some way of recognizing our self.

Existence is one thing - all that is - and when you find yourself on this level of knowing, there is no you.

The first time I experienced myself as something other than what I knew myself to be was about a year and a half after my first experience. Again it happened in that moment before sleep, only this time I was more awake than normal. I was tossing and turning in my bed and could not get comfortable, no matter what I did. Initially, I put it down to hormones, as these could make me feel restless and uncomfortable. Then the energy in the room changed. It became quite electric, and I was scared about what was going to happen, although I knew I was safe. It was the unknown that made me scared. My body was buzzing and vibrating and suddenly felt really heavy. Then I started to experience again the feeling that I was having a heart attack, but this time I did not fight it. I relaxed. What happened next happened so fast that I was blown away. The speed of the transition I went through was faster than time. It was as if I went backwards and forwards and stood still quicker than anything. I had nothing in my vocabulary to describe it other than to say it felt as if I was travelling at the speed of light. I was outside of my body and I was totally free, but I could still feel an attachment to this lump of meat that I thought I was. Being out of my body and becoming aware of it, my Earthly body felt so cold and unfeeling in comparison to this other me I was in. Yes, this new me, even though I'd just discovered it, was more familiar and real than the body I had spent my life in. So here I was, me, myself and I. I was all of a sudden aware of the mind, body and soul I was, but I also knew that there was more of me, which was even less of an identity than what I was experiencing my self to be in this moment.

This all happened so quickly and so smoothly. It felt unbelievable, yet I was so comfortable and accepting of it, because it was all so familiar. I was floating above my body, then I flipped over and my head was where my physical body's feet were. I was out of my body and knew I could go anywhere I wanted to. I decided to go and see my mom, because I knew if she saw me above her bed she wouldn't be afraid, as most people would. I could pay attention to what was in her room and I could verify it the next day. As I reached the window, I knew I did not have to open it, but then it occurred to me that I had no clothes on! In a flash, I was spinning above my body like a rotor on a helicopter. I started to panic. I couldn't get back into my body. What was I going to do? All of a sudden, two hands grabbed me around my waist and slipped me back into my body, pulled the covers over me and patted me like a baby. The hands were the same giant soft hands that were pulling my leg the last time. My eyes were open, I was wide awake, and I could still feel the energy all around me. When looking through my physical eyes, my view is so very limited. The eyes I had been looking out of saw everything, three hundred and sixty degrees around me. I could see whatever I thought of, as if there was no such thing as space or time. But I was now more accepting of these events. I turned over and went to sleep. My thoughts, while this was going on, were all about the fear I felt and how that fear had stopped me from going any further. Indeed, fear stops us so much in our physical life, and our astral existence.

Chapter 49

Now

Past, present and future are all the same thing. When you are sitting in your essence, it is all happening at once, as I have already explained regarding cause and effect. Time is what creates before, now and afterwards. Only when you are able to be fully present in the moment will you be able to fully understand what time is. Now (by this I mean the moment of now) is infinite, it has no beginning, no middle and no end. It just is.

Whenever we look into the future (daydream, plan ahead) or gaze into the past, we say that the past is provable and the future is not, because it has not happened yet. If we look back (within our memory) at an event that has happened from the moment we are now in, and we have received new information, which is different from what happened at the time of the event in the past, what happens to the past? It changes because of new information or observations. Everything that exists we only know to be because of our observation of it. We believe that the future does not yet exist. To have a future, we need to move forward, and the future can only exist when looking at it from the past. So both the future and the past are changeable because of thought, but the moment is not changeable. It can only be what it is; it only changes when looking back at it and thinking that it was a different future from the one you thought it would be.

So the only thing that is real and not changeable is the now moment. But our physical and Earthly mind only sees or knows the past to exist. This is to create some form of stability against which to measure. The future and the past exist in the moment of now within your true essence, because your observation point is different, (you are not be observing, just being as one). In the now moment, it feels as if you are observing life (as a human) from a faraway place, and the past and the future are sitting in front of you like movies being played simultaneously, interacting with each other. Imagine that your movie screen is sectioned into three. The first section is your past, the middle is your now, and the last section is your future. Then remove the sections and it is all interactive. One event has an effect on the others, but it is all happening at the same moment. Time and space sit in the moment of now and only exist because of the now moment. The moment of now can be found in or through time and space, yet it is free from both.

Chapter 50
Altered States

The reason we enter different states of reality is to discover how much more there is to being. Whatever state of reality/dimension you find your awareness in, the one place you are always in is in your essence. It is your essence that is your truth. There is no particular thing you have to do or age you need to be to connect to your essence. You are always connected; you do not exist if you are not. There are many events and stages of your life that make it easier to connect (become aware), but these are not essential. When you are on a road to discovery there is always a starting point. The discovery that you are seeking to make is a journey to yourself, so you need to start with you.

Learn to assess yourself by asking yourself questions about things that you took for granted. Start with a simple question such as, 'What do different colours mean to me?', 'What type of music really lifts my spirits?', 'What foods make me feel good?'. Start to find the you that you are now rather than living in the past. Pay attention, open your eyes and really look. Don't do anything without giving it your full attention. This is living in the moment. After a while you will realize that you are observing yourself in the moment, if you are paying full attention with your mind and body. This is your essence. Have you ever felt that you are being watched? This normally happens when you are really engrossed in something pleasurable and creative. This is your essence. By discovering that there is an aspect of you observing you from outside of your physical body, you start to realize that you are more than a body and a mind. Something only exists to you because you are observing it; if you look away you can no longer see it. But does that mean it has disappeared? Not really, because you are also observing it with your essence. There is a part of your being that sees things (knowing) that your body does not; it is your sixth sense. This is an observing sense, which is far more aware than your five physical senses. The reason for the sixth sense is to link your body and mind to your essence, just as your five senses link your body and mind to the Earth. By paying attention to the moment you are in, by being fully present with all your five senses, you will activate your sixth sense, which will open the door to your essence. This space that you are in after activating your sixth sense is a part of your essence. This is called an altered state of reality. I describe it as a part of your essence because you are a multidimensional being and you will have already discovered one part of those multidimensional levels. Everything that is around us in our everyday life is there to assist us on our journey of discovery of our truth. The journey is very pleasurable when you realize that it is a great adventure (your movie). By partaking in yoga, t'ai chi, meditation or any other similar practice, you will learn to be in the moment, which will assist you to discover your truth. But they do not themselves present the truth to you; they are simply tools to help you. Only you can discover your truth. This book and every thing I do with people can also be seen as a tool. By telling you of my experiences and how to live life in a way that makes you content and happy, my book is a great tool. But that is all it is to you, unless you use it to discover your essence. Then you will see it as the way to discover yourself. The information within these pages is very important and also a natural process in our journey through life.

You may have a full and happy life and feel that there is nothing missing, just as I did a few years ago. But there will come a time when you will experience something that is outside of your normal everyday life. How can I say that? Because of the knowing that I have discovered. This knowing has not made me a know-all; I am just more aware. That is why I have chosen a light-hearted approach. We take life too seriously most of the time, getting caught up in the dramas, not living and being.

Chapter 51
The Actor

So you are an actor in this movie called life. What part are you going to play next? Which drama scene are you going to choose in which to find pleasure or pain? Yes, this may sound unreal or even plain harsh, but your movie and the scenes you play are up to you the actor and you the director, who wrote the movie. To play your part the way you wrote it, you need to get in touch with that aspect of your nature. And to play the part, you, the actor, just have to follow your own direction. Please remember that you chose this life, so take responsibility for it and live it the way you want it to be. And the only part you are playing and directing is your own, so stop trying to control other people.

Whatever your movie is, it is a journey towards yourself. And this journey leads you to all the answers to all the questions you have about life and existence. There are infinite levels to our true being, so anything we have spent our time looking for or searching for, we already have. We are it. So why are we searching? As long as we see ourselves simply as human beings we will have to search for the rest. Once we discover this secret behind our humanness then and only then will we be able to play our role as a role in the life movie. I am aiming my sights high and would like to achieve a universal Oscar!

Chapter 52
Essence

When we, as an essence, die and leave this planet, we enter another reality. When I say leave, I do not mean we go to another place. I mean that our sense of self changes and we feel as if we are somewhere else. We also perceive ourselves in a totally different way. After entering another reality, we have work to do, and this work will depend on the reality we find ourselves in. Of these, there are zillions. When we have completed the work within this reality, we move on to the next and continue to do so until there is no reality. Reality only exists where we find ourselves to be. What I am really saying is that we grow through different experiences in different realties, until we reach a level where there is nothing. We cannot be defined for there is nothing to define us. We reach a point of nowhere, where there is nothing - no boundaries, no limits, no distinction. This is what is called all that is. It is a pure and simple nothing with the full potential to be anything or nothing. For all that is to become anything it thinks it into existence.

So thought is the creation and the material that is used is all that is. Even though thought itself is all that is. So there is nothing in existence that is it and nothing in existence that is not it, for it is everything and nothing at the same time (remembering that there is no such thing as time). You can see why we have such a hard job trying to understand ourselves as human beings, let alone what we truly are or are not.

Chapter 53
Guides and Helpers

Many people will tell you about their guides and helpers and all the many different forms they appear to them in. In an earlier chapter, when I was talking about blueprint higher consciousness, I said that it could present itself in many different ways. Well, guides and helpers were what I was talking about. They are all part of your own essence; they are an aspect of you. Although they appear to you as a separate entity, you have to remember that you are a multidimensional being and these helpers are from one of those dimensions. This will only be understood when you fully understand that there is only one: all that is.

At the start of my journey of discovery, I thought that the information or presence that I was receiving or seeing was something outside of me, definitely nothing to do with me personally. That was until I started to discover more and more of my essential being. You may not agree with this now, as it will depend on where you are in your own journey. The reason that these aspects of ourselves appear in this way is because when we are living as a human being we are seeing ourselves as a separate identity; so to communicate with ourselves, we use a separate identity. This makes us pay more attention to the information that we become aware of. If it were not presented to us in this way we would ignore our own wisdom or knowing, because we do not know ourselves to be anything other than the human being. We are all having different experiences within different dimensions and in different forms of being, all at the same time. There are also times when many aspects of us merge into one. And for you, this is one of those times. You are bringing these aspects of yourself together into your physical being; you are merging more with more of yourself. The people around you are here to do this too. We then end up with merged beings on the planet Earth and this has a cause and an effect, for the better, I might add.

So we will merge with higher aspects of ourselves; some of those aspects are the same aspects in the people around you. You will be able to see that aspect of yourself that sits in you and in other people, for it will have no separation. This is when you will see yourself in others and you will treat these people the way you would treat yourself, which is with love, truth and kindness. Because for you to be able to see this aspect of yourself in them, you will have reached a stage in your journey where it would be impossible for you to see yourself or them in any other way.

It took me a long time to realize that the being that pulled my leg and the being that put me back into my body was actually me. It was also another part of me that, when I was out of my physical body, I was more aware of. It was the protector me, the mother me. On a grander scale, it was the guiding me, and this me was funny, gentle and extremely large. It had a more male feel to it, so it was the father and the mother of myself.

We are all aware of aspects of our self in a physical sense - the bitch me, for example, or the kind me, the hormonal me. Well, this is the same on all other levels of awareness. There are many parts that make the whole.

Chapter 54
Levels

There are many levels that we go through on our journey to ourselves. Each of these levels has many stages and each of these levels has awareness. We need to understand these and then incorporate them into our being before we are able to live them in their truth. In other words, each level and the many stages in that level need to be absorbed in order for us to know them and live them. These levels unfold naturally; there is no time process or age attachment to them.

Some people never forget their essence from birth, but do not know how to live this truth in a physical way. Each level has to be worked through. But everyone is different and one person might only need to work on one stage at level one, whereas another person might need to work on six stages at level one. The amount of work you do on each stage will depend on your contract (what you came here to do), your facility at letting go and how much work you put into it. So you might find that level one takes you two years to fully complete and absorb, whereas level two only takes you two minutes. But to be able to live the life and be the being you are designed to live and be, you will have to go through all the levels, one way or another. You can learn these levels by experiencing them in a dramatic way; you can simply go with the flow, fight or think your way through. When I say that you need to work through each level, I am not saying that there is coursework to do. The work happens naturally once you are on your path. It unfolds. It is definitely a process that we will all experience. How fast depends on how quickly you learn. The levels are what you might know as auras, philosophies or religious practices. But they are all there to assist you to be the true being that you are.

The first level is all about your sense of belonging in a physical way; the family you come from, the sex you are and your understanding of it, the tribe/country you are born into, and the race you belong to.

The second level is connected to your sexuality and your roles within your gender. This level is your connection to others and your relationships.

The third level is about the discovery of yourself as a human being and your connection to the world outside of you, your feeling and place in your own unique world inside of you.

The fourth level is your love. When you discover love on many different levels you are ready to discover more of yourself. It is a very important level; it is the connection level between the Earth you and the higher you.

The fifth level is your communication level - this is the voice that represents you, including your presence. This level is probably the most used level, for it is the way we communicate on a physical level. It allows you the ability to convert what you are aware of on higher levels down to an understandable Earth level. It is the level that I am using now and, because I am a teacher on all levels, I use this level all the time.

The sixth level is seeing things clearly - not only with your eyes but also with your sixth sense. It is a form of visualization that has a language all of its own.

The seventh level is where you are aware of your humanness being more than you once knew it to be. This level has the most stages to it, for it has many different truths. This is because it is the connection to all that is. This level is open to anything and everything. So your truth sits within each stage you are working on within this level. It changes as you move to the next stage. This is quite complex, although very simple when you are in the knowing aspect of your essence.

There are many more levels after the seventh and they are normally active if you are here to teach this way of being. There are other levels between the ones I have mentioned, but they interact with the main ones. I am sure this information has made you think that there is too much work to do. Well, most of this work you are doing without being aware of it. This information is there as a guide to assist you when you feel you are stuck. Each of these levels is normally associated with a certain area of the body. Pain around the chest area is linked to love - either you're in need of it or your need to project it.

The first level is at the base of your spine, the second is below your navel, the third above your navel. The fourth is in the chest area, the fifth around the throat, the sixth in the middle of your forehead and the seventh at the crown. So when you are working on certain problems in your life, see where you are feeling that problem and connect it to the work in that area. These are basic guides to assist you, they are not rules or part of natural law. But your body does talk to you, and if you take the time to listen then these areas will serve as communication between you and your body.

Chapter 55
Memory

When we enter this planet through the birthing process, we have no memory; our memory as we know it is attained by living a physical life. But we do have another type of memory, which is knowing. This is not a cellular memory; it is the memory of essence. While we are babies this is the only thing we are aware of. We now find ourselves (not knowing ourselves to be a self at this time) being contained and not able to communicate. We have to learn how to be a self, for there is no such thing in our essence; it is alien to us. We do not know how to be this body we find ourselves in. As this body grows through its preordained stages (DNA) and with the assistance of our parents/guardians, we learn how to use our body. Then we learn how to communicate by using our mind and body, which are the physical tools we are equipped with. The more we learn with our physical body and mind, the less we use our essence memory, because its use is never encouraged and there appears to be no instrument or tool in this body to express it.

Our essence is capable of anything it desires; it has no barriers or restrictions as the body does. The essence has no conflicts with itself or anything else, for there is nothing other than itself. There comes a point in our life when our essence memory is able to find an outlet in the body. It is not a particular part of the body, it is more an all-over awareness. This awareness feels as if it is something other than you, it feels alien to you - that is, the you that you now know yourself to be. But the truth is that this is you in your essence. Remember that your essence can be anything it wishes to be. So what actually happens is that we go full circle. We are essence, and then we find ourselves as a self, contained in a body/mind. We learn to be this body/mind so well that we believe ourselves to be it alone. Then we discover something or other outside of this body and learn all about it, only to discover that it was us all along, being whatever we wanted to be. Quite bizarre, really!

No wonder it takes us a long time to figure it all out. This is the point when we know what we are doing here and why; who we find ourselves to be and what we are doing here with this body/mind. Yes, the contract, the movie you wanted to play a part in, becomes clear. At this point of your journey it will all make sense to you.

Then comes the hardest bit of all. You now know yourself to be something more than this body/mind but you still have to continue on your journey. At this point, most people would want to stop being something they are not and go home. You came here to do and be what it it is not possible for you to truly be, unless you believed yourself to be a separate identity.

So everything that we can do on this planet, in this body, with other people, is a pleasure and honour and a great discovery to us as an essence. When you reach this point, please remember this and you will learn how to bring more of your essence into your physical reality. This will make your movie the best it can possibly be.

Chapter 56
Easier Said than Done

Easier said than done - what is this all about? This statement I find to be such a contradiction because of how I now see life and know life to be. This chapter would have been left out of the book but for my wonderful sister Karen, who has bounced backwards and forwards on her journey to herself and quotes this to me all the time. So let's work with it.

If something is easy to say but not easy to do, why is this so? Saying something is the same as doing something in my book, but this is not always the case. We create with our thoughts, but to create something tangible we have to put those thoughts into action. So, to say something and then say that it is not easily done is to imply that one is capable of thought but not capable of creating that thought and making it a reality. This means that someone saying this thinks way beyond what they believe themselves capable of achieving, or else the person telling them what they could do has more faith in their ability than they do in themselves. Once you discover that thought is creative, you would expect to turn that thought into creation. Otherwise why think the thought in the first place? Okay, there is wishful thinking, which is part of hope. Hope is not very creative; it is relying on a source outside of ourselves to make something happen. Hope also resides in fear, and fear is what stops us from realizing our full potential. Dreams are a different story from thoughts. Dreams are by design and just that. They are not meant to be turned into a reality. They are freedom of thought with no responsibility attached. This includes daydreams. If there was something you would like to do or to be, then discover a way to make it a reality. And if you spend your day wishful thinking, then it is about time you took action. Let go of the fear, and try. You never know, you might discover a new you that has been waiting to appear. Taking responsibility for one's thoughts and actions is living one's truth. There is no better way to live.

I discovered so many new aspects of myself that the problem became what I was going to do with this new person. I needed an outlet to express my truth. I thought about training. What could I do to get the certificate on the wall? What qualification did I need to do what I was really good at? But there was nothing out there that taught what I knew and no qualification to be had that allowed me the freedom of expression I required. This of course led me to the point of creating a new philosophy, with a truth that had always been there and a fresh way of understanding life and beyond. My thoughts desperately needed to be put into action. And in order for that to happen, I needed a description or a title for what I was going to give to the world. I went from healer, to light worker, to spiritual counsellor, but nothing seemed to fit. The nearest I have got is 'spiritual life coach', but even this is not quite right. The main reason for this is that to label is to limit, and the work I do has no limits. I work with every kind of problem or situation that people find themselves in. My main aim is to get them to discover their truth. So maybe I am a truth coach or a truth seer. One day I might find a description that fits, but I grow daily and I have new awareness to teach all the time. Each new awareness leads me in a new direction so, for now, I am a freedom teacher.

Chapter 57
Responsibility

Taking responsibility for your life and your actions is the most powerful and rewarding gift that you could possibly give to yourself and those people around you. When we reach this point in our journey, we start to live life more consciously and make wiser decisions. Also, by being responsible you have a link to many other aspects of your being.

What is responsibility? It is knowing that each of your actions causes an action or reaction, being fully aware of the outcome, and accountable for it. If you were able at this moment to see and know yourself within a different reality, you would be aware that everything is visible, even though you would not be able to lie or pretend, for everyone around you would know.

So if you were to live your life like this in your Earth reality, you would be living your truth and taking responsibility for yourself and your creations, whether these are thoughts or actions. As a human being, everything we do, say or think has a cause and an effect. By understanding and owning this, you are being responsible.

Chapter 58

Freedom

We all want or would like to be free, but free from what? This is the question. Are we not free, or is it that we simply act as if we are not free? Do we feel constrained, imprisoned or restricted?

All of this implies that we are not free, and this is true up to a point. So many people tell me that they just want to be themselves; but they feel unable to do this for one reason or another. No one is stopping you from being you; no one has the key to your prison, only you. All of the restrictions are self-imposed - they are your illusions. To remove these illusions you need to walk and talk your truth; you need to present you and the way you know yourself to be. To walk and talk your truth you have to discover it, so, as I have mentioned earlier, you have to look at everything around you, including yourself, and discover what you feel or think or know. Then, when you have done this, you can walk and talk your truth. Once you start being this true you, there is a sense of freedom, which grows as you discover more and more of your true nature. Whatever situation you find yourself in, you can always do this. If you are in prison, in an unhappy relationship, in grief because you have lost a loved one, you are always free to be. An outside obstacle might restrict your physical body but your being is always free to be. Once you know that your being is always free, no matter what is going on around you, you are on the road to you. The old saying, 'you cannot break his spirit', is so true; all you have to do is know that it is there and that it is you. This is true freedom of being.

Chapter 59
Paranormal

Thousands of people experience all kinds of different phenomena and yet to prove what they experience is almost impossible. The one thing that is remarkable about these people is that although they come from all walks of life, there is almost always honesty about them, and a strength of conviction that is so strong that they are willing to suffer any form of rebuttal. The reason that they cannot prove what they know is because it is not as yet part of our proverbial scientific understanding. There are many things that are not really part of this scientific understanding that we have on planet Earth. Because they are not explicable in what we term a realistic manner, they do not exist. Love is one of the things that defy science. You can see the cause and the effects of love: pupils dilating, an increased pulse rate, cheeks blushing. These are similar effects to those reported by someone who is experiencing the paranormal. We can measure the cause and the effect, but not witness the experience. Does this mean that it is not happening?

We all know what love is, and no one out there would be able to tell us that we are not in love. For love is a knowing that is individual to us all. So is the paranormal. Love is not known by mind. Sadness is not known by touch. Rejection is not known by taste. All of these comments tell us that there are lots of different parts to us that are able to experience things, things that they are designed to know. The reason we have a problem with the paranormal is that we are trying to know it with a part of our being that was not designed for this level of understanding. What happens to people who experience the paranormal (and here I include myself) is that they enter a different level of awareness that can only be accessed in their own energy vibration field. It is within this level that there are many other realities and non-realities, which is the only description I can find for other awareness within other dimensions of real and unreal existence - real meaning separate, outlined identity, unreal meaning not having an outline or being definable. But both of these real and non-real vibrations exist to those people who can use their sixth-sense awareness. This awareness has many levels, and each of these levels is different.

I have had numerous different types of paranormal experiences and I have met many people who have experienced at least one or two different types of paranormal events during their lifetimes. The fact that I have 'been there' gives them a sense of relief, comforts them and reassures them that they are not going mad! I can help them discover the truth behind such an experience. Most people make a mistake in becoming so attached to this event that nothing else in their life has much meaning any more. I help them to get back to living a full life. I do this not by denying their experience, but by understanding it. Then their life takes on a new direction of discovery.

Chapter 60
Immunity

To do this kind of work you reach a point where you become immune to the physical world, whilst at the same time being in it and of it. Sounds crazy, I know, but it is the only way I can describe what will happen or what you need to do. To find this immunity, you need to be aware of the bigger picture, and it takes a type of immunity to understand that. Yes, another 'Catch-22' situation. Sorry, but remember that life is a contradiction because we have opposite polarities.

So, the bigger picture is that you are more than the physical being that you know yourself to be. To really know this, you need to lose any preconceived ideas you have of your being. This allows you a sense of freedom. Once you follow through with this freedom, it is able to unfold and you are able to discover more and more about yourself. While this is happening, you start to disassociate from the you that you were. This is the start of your immunity. This happens not long after you have reached the place where you ask yourself what's the point. This immunity is more a freedom to see and know life and your place within it in a different light. It is a form of non-attachment, which is required to get you to the next stage of your being.

This stage can be very scary, however, because once you are immune you cannot see the point to being alive. For, at this stage, materialism has no place. Relationships are things that were part of the old you and are not needed at this moment. You have no needs, no reason, no understanding of where you are or even what you are. This is what many people call the dark night of the soul. In fact, it is the dark night of our humanness and the freedom of the soul. It is a form of dying of your humanness or of the ego self. This is required for you to grow on other levels. You do not lose yourself; you will discover more of your self, but the old values and reasons you had before certainly will change. This process is a form of metamorphism - the human into the being.

To me, it was more like a step beyond the illusion that I knew as my life. This process can last a few days at most, but generally it is one day or a matter of hours. Getting to this point can take quite some time. This is not something to fear; it is a wonderful stage of crossing from one stage to another. Once you are over the immune stage, you see life and even death differently. It is looking at the world with new eyes that see things clearly. Suddenly, everything makes sense to you. You can't believe how you previously missed this truth - it is so obvious. Then this immunity turns into a form of connection to everything and the relationships you have now have more value than you thought was possible, only now they are free and not needy.

I personally feel that people need assistance through this stage, as it is a moment of being lost. If you are not aware that you will find yourself again, it can be very scary. I speak from experience.

Chapter 61

Common Sense

Most of the things that I write about in this book you would say are simply common sense, and you are right. Common sense is a sense just like hearing and seeing, only it does not have a part of the body where you can say it belongs. It comes from your mind. We all know common sense, albeit in different degrees. It is common to all; it is a unity within all of us. So if what I am saying makes sense, it is because it is a truth that is part of us all. There will be certain things that do not make sense to you at this moment, but they will as you read further. I am not saying mine is the only truth, but that there is truth in these words. It is your common sense that knows this truth.

Chapter 62
The Hard Way or the Easy Way

How many times have you heard people say, 'I always have to learn things the hard way' or 'If there is a hard way, I will find it'?

To learn a particular thing the hard way is to say that there is an easier way. So why would we not choose the easy way? Human nature is basically lazy and we like things to be easy. Yet we often make things hard for ourselves. I think that the truth is that it makes everything more real. Maybe by making life easy, it will break the illusion we have created. Remember that we created this illusion to experience what is not possible unless we know this life we live to be real and of value. So we signed up for an experience that allowed us to do and be many things, and this is only possible if it feels real. The harder it is, the more real it feels.

On our journey, there are many things that we want to experience before we move on to the next stage, which is self-realization. For at this stage/level there is the opportunity to discover more of our truth. It is like observing ourselves from a distance and seeing the consequences of our actions. When I reached this stage of being, it was strange watching people around me doing things the hard way, suffering when there was no need to. I tried to tell them, but they were unable adopt the easier way. It was impossible for them, for they required this experience as part of their contract or because they were co-creating with their free will. It was something that they chose to know for their own growth. It is very hard to see and know what a person is about to go through. You want to protect them or make it easy for them, but you cannot - it is their way, for them.

All of you parents out there will know what I am talking about. No matter how much you try to tell your children about the consequences of their actions, they still have to try it for themselves. When you reach the stage of self-realization, you feel like a parent to the world, and most of the time you can do nothing to help. All you can do is tell people what you know; the rest is up to them. This is a hard stage because if you suddenly know all of these things and yet cannot pass them on, what is the point of knowing? The answer is that we can help people to get to know themselves and this will have a knock-on effect.

So, to recap, in life we often choose the hard way in order to feel that we are truly living. Sounds odd, I know, but by taking part in suffering, grief, anger or frustration, you get more real all the time. Our first role on this planet is to know ourself as a real separate being.

Chapter 63
Teachers and Students

Every single person that I have met on my journey has been my teacher or my student in one way or another. The people who come to me for my wisdom are both my teachers and my students. The information they require is part of my higher consciousness. I simply need to step this down to a physical level for them to understand. It is part of my knowing that is all around me like an immense library and available to be tuned into at any time by anyone. The fact that you are reading this book allows me to be the teacher and you the student. So to write this book I have had to be the student and the teacher at the same time.

Two-way communication is the key. There are no teachers without students, and when a student knows his truth, he becomes the teacher. The reason I know all I know is because other people wanted to know more and more. Yes, in the beginning I was the person who needed to know what was happening to me, so I went on a voyage of discovery and learnt what I required. Since then all the other knowing has been because of others needs, for which I am truly grateful, because it has assisted me.

Spiritual intelligence is very different from IQ. IQ is Earth intelligence, which is measured by another being or exams set by a group of people outside of you. It is based on your ability, memory and recall of information, as well as techniques that you have learnt. With spiritual intelligence, it is a different story, for it is truth and there is only one truth. Spiritual information is not stored; it is just there, as and when it is required. Once it has been given (the passing on of information), it enters our memory. So if a person is eloquent, this will assist in their competent communication of the truth. Because there are so many different levels of awareness, where you find your attention will influence the truth of that level/dimension. So, to be the kind of teacher and student I am suggesting, all that is required is that you reach a level on Earth where you are able to communicate effectively. Then you need to find your truth to access the universal library.

When people start to do this work, they are always told that the teacher will be there when the student is ready. The mistake they make is that they look for some mystical being to arrive. When everyone you meet is your teacher, this can appear in a positive or a negative way. The important thing is to learn the lesson that is being taught.

To be a teacher can at times be frustrating. You have the answers to questions that people ask and all you can give them is tools to help them live their life in a better way for them. However, frustration can result from having to explain the same thing over and over again.

Chapter 64

Lonely and Alone

I would like you to think about what these two words mean to you and take your self to a time when you really felt lonely and then one when you felt alone.

'Leave me alone, I want to be alone.' These statements are saying that I would like time with this person called I. What leads us to reach this stage? Well, this is what we are doing here on this planet, in this body. Yes, we are here to discover what it is like to be a separate identity, and the one sure way of doing this is to be alone. Some people have chosen to truly know what it feels like to be alone. I am talking about those who choose to sail the world single-handed or, say, live as a recluse. This may seem a strange choice to make, but these people have no distractions other than to stay alive and be with themselves.

Remember, whenever you find yourself wanting to be alone, it is being with you that you are choosing. It is a great opportunity to really get to know yourself and discover your limits, even risk going beyond them, daring to be more than you thought you were or discovering that on a physical level you are not as capable as you thought. It is all about your truth on a level that, though you live with it every day, you never take the time or space to know. If you are alone for long periods of time, you will automatically start to find a new way of seeing and understanding life. This is all for your personal growth. Don't start feeling sorry for yourself; this will only cause you to stagnate.

Loneliness is a state of mind that is consuming. It is a place that we reach with reluctance and despair. When we are lonely we feel that the world has nothing for us; it feels like a continuously dark place in which we simply exist. Loneliness makes us feel that we are lost; we do not know what to do to find a bit of happiness. Loneliness can, however, be a tool, and a very powerful tool at that. For it is a moment of freedom. The loneliness I am referring to in this instance is when anything outside of you has no meaning or no purpose. If you use this time to look within, you will discover yourself on a physical level, getting to know the person you are, rather than who you think you are. You will begin an adventure that will blow your mind. In doing this, your loneliness becomes aloneness and you are able to enjoy the you that you are getting to know. Then, when you feel ready, the world will come calling because the energy you will be projecting will be bright and attractive. Loneliness is being bored with who you are. When you take the time to discover the true you and start loving the being you are, then loneliness is gone forever. Being alone is something we will continue to choose every now and again because we like to think of ourselves as a separate identity. The loneliness I was going through when I started to get to know myself was caused by the fact that I was not sharing myself with other people. This was through fear. I thought that other people would think that I was crazy; maybe they did and still do. But since I dared to be myself, I have certainly never felt lonely.

Chapter 65
Life after Death

This is probably one of the fascinating topics for the human race. Do we continue to exist in some form after we have died? The answer is yes, but to know this for sure is what is difficult. We all want proof, and the proof we require is physical evidence. It is impossible to prove your existence on a physical level when you are not in that reality. Once the body has stopped functioning, what is left is the energy that gave it the opportunity to be human. This energy is not the same as the energies we use and measure within the laws of nature of the planet Earth. Its vibration is more refined - so fast that it appears not to exist, too delicate for our five physical senses to pick up. Our physical senses do not feel or understand these vibrations by design. They are there in order for us to know ourselves as separate. The other sense we have is aware of these vibrations and knows them to be a truth on another level.

So the only possible way to know that we continue to exist after physical death is to use the sixth sense we have. This is our access to all knowing, and it is capable of understanding on many different levels of awareness. The problem we have with this extra sense is converting it into human vibration understanding, as I am trying to do. The reason that we don't use this ability of our sixth sense is that it is not part of this reality as yet. This is because we do not have any help in learning to express and really understand what is going on with our intuitive sixth sense. This knowing is always there and always has been. The real reason we do not choose it is because we want to experience being a human being fully.

The next stage of humanity is going to be a more realized being, which is what the next two thousand years are all about. Yes, this is evolution of the human species. I know this sounds a little bit off the wall, but I can only explain it this way. We have always evolved and we will continue to do so, only now we have reached the ultimate reality.

We will be evolving backwards, not to where we have just been, but in a circle going back to the starting point. This will become clearer as we proceed a little further along our shared path.

Back to life after death. There is existence, but not as a separate identity, more as a thought form that can think its self into a form of reality. It thinks, so it is. There is a merger that happens when we die, and this merger is a joining of soul energy, which still has the ability to know and be at any moment a separate thought experience. Of course, the experience is down to the thought. We have a hard job understanding this because we exist in time and space. So our thoughts take time to develop. This merger that happens after we die feels like going home. It is freedom from being and becoming one with life. Not life as we know it. You still have reason, but desire starts to disappear, as you are aware that you can be or have anything you want. This stops the need. You become more inquiring as to the nature of the awareness you have, but you know that it is your thought that created it. After you leave your physical sense of being you remember, and this remembering is the same as what we can do with our sixth sense. This is why I can tell you about life after death. But please realize that these are the thoughts that I allow myself to know. I have learnt that it is our thoughts that create the reality, so I have taught myself not to think while being in my sixth sense. This allows me a sense of freedom to observe, but as soon as I think about what I am aware of it stops. I find the truth behind everything by not being even a thought. Then I try my best to give description to experience without thought. It is our thought process that keeps us tied up to the reality we find our thoughts within. As complex as it sounds, it is so simple that it is scary. What we think is what is. So stop thinking and you discover the truth.

Today you may have noticed that young children are expressing their sixth sense and their parents are starting to listen to them. For anything to evolve on this planet takes time. Everything that has happened has been part of a process that leads us to activate our next stage of being. Today, we have laws in place to protect our right to freedom of speech, and without this there would be stagnation. Our right to freedom leads us to discover for ourselves. So use the abilities you have and start discovering the person you are, the planet you live on and the reason for it all. This will send you on a journey of great discovery that will absolutely amaze you.

Chapter 66
True Self

I am always asked, 'What do I have to do to be my true self?' Well, the answer is just be you. This is confusing because people tend to think that they were already being their true selves. They don't know what their truth really is. To be who you truly are, you need to discover you.

What people really need to know is how to remove what they are not. What you are not is the outer layers of life experiences that you have attached to yourself and made you. So to start, you must remove the illusion of you, after which you are left with the real you. This all sounds very easy, and trust me, it is. The hard part is recognizing yourself without the illusion. The illusion is 'I am good at', 'I am pretty', 'I am sad'. These are expressions of the you which you believe yourself to be as a result of experiences, information and teaching you have had so far. We represent ourselves with many different things but we are not them: 'I am strong', 'I am hard working', 'I am emotional'. We define ourselves through the work we do or the role we play; mother, husband, accountant, lawyer, comedian, whatever. We are programmed throughout our lives to define and be something outside of ourselves. We have become what we do in life, not who we are. And we get scared when we start to remove the layers, for if we are not all of the things we know ourselves to be, then what are we?

You are like a present that is wrapped up with pretty bows and nice paper. You open the wrapping, untie the bow and inside there is a box. You open it. There is another box. You open this. Yet another box - this is fun! Then you open the next box. Ah! You understand what is going on now. Someone wants to disguise the true nature of the present. Then you open the next box and there is another box, only now they are getting smaller and you suspect that maybe it is not going to be such a good gift after all. But you continue to unwrap. Damn! There is another box inside this one and you decide that this is getting boring. You open this box and now the present is wrapped in newspaper. Everyone is watching you and you are going to hate it if it is a joke. You rip off the paper and there is another tiny box. This has to be the last one as it is too small to get anything more inside it. At this point you are scared and excited at the same time. What if there is nothing in there? How disappointed you will be. What if it is what you have always wanted? Will you be able to cope with the emotion of it? All you have to do now is open it and you will know the truth of what is in there.

Oh! You want me to tell you; you don't want to have to discover it for yourself.

Well, I can tell you what was in my tiny box but I cannot tell you what is in yours. I opened the tiny box and found a loose ball of tissue paper. I slowly unwrapped the paper and inside was the most beautiful, perfect, sparkling diamond I had ever seen. It was so overwhelming I could not believe what I was seeing. I cried with joy.

Have you worked out what the present is yet?

Yes, it is you!

I have spent many years opening layers upon layers of my self and my life and I keep finding different facets of this diamond and how all of them together represent a truth that is I and beyond me.

Chapter 67
Lying

What is it that makes us lie? What reason do we have to lie? When I was a little girl one of my biggest shocks was the discovery that adults told lies. I was being taught to tell the truth. I thought that it was only children who lied and that when I was all grown up, I would not lie any more. I have spent many hours trying to discover why we lie.

Not really. In truth, I have spent about half an hour looking at the reasons for lying. Saying I spent hours, rather than telling the truth, gives my writing more value. Or does it? Is it not valuable because of how little time it took? In our society we feel that we must justify ourselves, and for some reason time allotted is a form of worth. So the first set of lies we fall for is exaggeration, for the sake of appreciation. There are many different forms of lying. We all forgive and accept exaggeration, but it is detrimental to us for it is not our truth.

Next, we come to manipulation. This form of lying may be used to try to control or to protect. Parents use manipulation all the time to try to help their offspring survive life and its pitfalls. They tell how they knew someone who did what you are considering doing and the consequences of that action. This is lying to protect, and again we accept this form of lying. If, however, we tell our children the truth, then we are teaching them one of the best things in life. We need to teach them that people do lie, and why. As parents we can give them the tools to assist them, then they can go out into the world and discover life for themselves. After all, that is what they are doing here.

The second type of manipulation through lying is power based. When people lie to obtain money, or to misrepresent something as a truth, this is manipulation. If you just take the time to look around, you will see how much manipulation there is in our world.

The next type of lying happens because people are not proud of who they are, so they pretend to be someone else. They deceive people

144

and themselves in order to have a better life. If they do not like who they are or what they do, then they need to change these things about themselves, rather than lie. They will then turn their lives around and perhaps become what they pretended to be, but without the lie.

All of these lies are falsehoods; the reasons behind them are different but they are still lies. Okay, I know that we are not saints as yet! But these lies have an effect on us all and they interfere with our connection to our true nature. We all lie at times because we believe ourselves to be this or that, when in truth we know we are none of these things. So, lying starts with the process of birth, and it takes many years of discovery and learning to understand that we are living a half-truth, which means that we are living a half-lie. So you could say that we are born liars, or living lies. When you reach the part in your journey of self-realization, this is the moment you discover the lie you have been living. And here is the funny thing. It was by design - you had no choice in the matter. This is the moment when you start to live more of your truth, and lies are no longer a big part of your life. The reason you no longer need to lie is because you have discovered a truth that is yours, and the respect you have for yourself and others is amazing. When you reach this stage there is nothing to hide, nothing you need in a true sense, so you have no reason to deceive. You now know that you are an essence reflection, shining through body and mind - and what could beat that?

You may think by now that what I am talking about is how to become a saint. Please believe me, this it is not so. My book, *Our Secret Movie*, is about discovering you; all of you - the good, the bad and the ugly.

It is not easy living your truth but it is oh so rewarding in the end. I found that I wanted to tell the truth about all kinds of different things. We know that we sometimes tell a white lie to protect. No longer having to do this was changing my personality and I was running the risk of being disliked. I had a choice to make and it was not an easy one. The work I do means that most of the time I tell people things that might hurt them. I really don't want to have to do this but if I don't tell the truth as I see it, then I suffer. I get frustrated with myself because I protected them from their self or their truth. But I found that there was still a part of myself that wanted to be loved by those around me.

The choice I had to make was between them and I, and although this felt selfish, I chose myself.

My life did not feel right when I chose not to speak my truth, so I went for it. In the beginning I felt kind of guilty; I still do in fact, on occasions. But the more I spoke my truth in a kind and loving way, the more results I achieved with the people I was helping, and this encouraged me to continue. When someone visits me for the first time, it might be hard for them to face so much truth, but most of the time I deliver it with a sense of humour, so they don't fight it and they soon find it refreshing. My truth is always delivered with love and there is no malice in my truth, only assistance.

Chapter 68
Needs

When we were born we required our parents/guardians to supply and meet our every need. If these needs were not met, we learnt ways to assist our getting what we wanted by crying, smiling, screaming, not sleeping, etc. Then, as we grow, we learn more ways to get what we want and what we require from the people around us. We also learn to do things for ourselves. This is living and learning. It is how we develop and grow to adapt to our world. These are the layers we now have to examine.

If we were lucky enough to be reared by people who knew the truth about life (mind, body and soul connection) then there would be far fewer layers to look at and examine. So the process of finding our essence or true self will have a lot to do with our upbringing, and the different ways of manipulation we used to get to where we are now.

To be you, who you know yourself to be, you are always thinking or doing something. The reason for this is that you are defining yourself through what you do. You are creating the person you call you. This is totally by design; it was the only way you could and would survive. To get to know your essence, you will need to stop defining who you are and start to get to know yourself by being in the moment. Taking every moment as fresh and new, not knowing and seeing life and yourself as the pattern you created throughout your life to make it easier.

This book is constantly giving you examples of everyday situations you live or come across and take for granted. What I am asking you to do is stop saying 'I have done that', 'I have been there', 'I did that in my first school'. We miss out on so much of life because we ignore the small things, and instead live in the past or the future. The moment is the place where you are. There is no past, for it has gone, and there is no future, for it is not here yet. So what I am saying to you is, you don't need to do anything to be you. But in order to be you, you need to remove the lifetime of stuff that you thought was you.

Up to the point in life when you started your journey to your true self, you were being your needs. So clean out the cupboards of your being and only put back in them what you really cannot live without. And when you have made space, you can be in that space doing nothing but being, and that is where you are.

Chapter 69

Outside Inside

When we are inside something looking out, we see everything outside of this place. The observation point we find ourselves to be in limits our vision and perception. But when we are on the outside of something looking in, we see a greater, bigger picture, for we are able to see the inside and the outside, as well as all around.

Picture yourself standing in a room with a door to the outside. All you can see is the room you are in and the view in front of you. Then view it from some distance away, outside. Now you can see a bigger picture - you can see where the room is and what it is part of, and what is behind, in front and to both sides of it. If I told you that who you truly are is inside of you, you would do your best to get inside any way you could. This is not what is required, and yet we are always taught that it is the inside where our truth is. This is only part of the picture. You exist inside and outside of yourself. So you need to observe yourself from a distance, so you get to see the bigger picture. This is confusing because there are so many levels or dimensions to our true existence that you will never be able to be outside of your true self. But you can observe the physical aspect of you, from another level. The way that we do this is by looking at our actions and reactions to life's situations. So we are observing from the inside looking at the outside. When we have realized by doing this that we are not our actions or reactions, then we cannot be on the outside of our self. So we are inside our being. The next thing that we can do is ask ourselves what part of us is observing us being us. This is the outside looking in, and what is it that is making that observation? It is another aspect of you that has been observing you all the time. It is hard to pick this up, but when you are busy doing something that takes all of your concentration, you may become aware of the sensation that you are being watched. This is you that is watching you.

Okay, I know that the mind is capable of doing lots of things at the same time, but this is different. You have a very real sensation that there is someone standing behind you. It is so strong that you turn around to see who is there. Being able to observe yourself means that you can tune into the part of yourself that sees a much bigger picture. The effects will amaze you. You start to understand things better. You understand things that you don't remember learning; you start to say things that are so very wise, and yet you don't know where they come from. And the more you do this, the more you become connected to the other part of you. This is different from normal learning - it is universal. By observing life from this point, you will have an easier and happier time whatever comes your way.

This process I have just explained is so easy (when you know how). But if you sit there and try to watch yourself it will not happen. Once you try you have failed; trying will only ever be that, whereas being is what is required. So you need to be fully present in a moment to free yourself from it. Then you are being and observing. The quickest way to be fully present is to be engrossed totally in what you are doing, as I have already said.

I was talking to my sister and her great friend Shazie on the phone yesterday. They both have found the secret to life and yet have lost it many times! By assisting these two, I learn new ways of explaining how they are to live their truth. What we discovered yesterday was that to discover this magnificence that is you, you go up to meet it. This is because it feels as if it is way above your head. What Shazie was not doing was bringing that magnificence down into her everyday life. She was escaping her humanness by going to her solitude, while in her essence. There would be no way she could hold on to this truth. This simple bit of information suddenly made all the difference to Shazie. She could see why she could not hold on to it. When you go to this space, this space where your truth lies, it is so beautiful. It is like a secret garden where you are the caretaker. Although you would love nothing more than to share it with people, you know that they have to find their path to it.

What I teach is not how to escape your life, but how to embrace your life and live it to its full capacity. To observe yourself, you will need to go beyond the self. So, take yourself out of the situation you are in and look at it from a distance and then live it with this new discovery. It is there all the time but we get so caught up in our situations that we cannot see the obvious.

Chapter 70
Strange Experiences

Over the last few years, I have had many different types of strange experience, some so bizarre that if I told you about them you would think that I am off my trolley. Believe me, there have been times when I thought I had truly lost my mind, but I now know why all of these different things happened, and more importantly what they mean. Some of them were presented to me in strange ways so I could not simply fob them off as imagination. All of the experiences were there to show me the array of different realities to existence.

There is only one way on this planet for us to truly know something and that is to experience it for ourselves, then there is no doubt. Sorry, I have to correct this: even when we experience something we still have to try to make it fit with what we already know life to be. And this is a good thing to do. So when we keep reaching the point where there is no Earthly explanation for what has happened, what do we do then?

Well, what I did was accept it for what it was, and then things started to change. The experiences made sense to me in a symbolic way. I am mentioning this here to help all of you who are going through similar things. No, you are not mad; just accept that this is within another reality. So, of course, it doesn't make sense or is alien to us. But it is as real as you and me, and that is as real as it gets! I will explain later.

It always helps to talk about these things, but please choose a friend who trusts you and knows you well. They don't have to agree with you; they are there so you can talk.

Have you ever been at a party or gathering and one person talks about a strange event in their life? Then almost all the other people in the room start revealing what had happened to them. It's as if they have been waiting for this moment all of their lives and they can't contain it any longer. All of the people who told their truth, revealed themselves, even at the cost of people not believing them, would have gone home and said that they had a really great night out. The reason is because they dared to go there. Because other people had similar experiences, they felt normal and part of a united front.

If you cannot tell anyone about what you have experienced, then write it down, keep a journal. It will be of value to your personal growth as you move on through your journey.

In the beginning I felt there were only a few people I could tell about what was happening to me. This time was so frustrating because all I wanted to talk about was this. I was living a life that felt false. I would be with friends and someone would mention something that appeared strange, and the response of other people around would be 'what a load of codswallop' or 'utter rubbish'. These comments stopped me from expressing what was happening to me. Why is this type of thing so easily dismissed, and why do we have to risk ridicule or persecution because we have experienced something that others haven't? I knew that I had to make it safe for me to be able to express my experience, but how could I do this?

I discovered that the only way was for the strange to become part of normal living experience, for it to be accepted. I know that it was the bizarreness of it all that people who had not had a personal experience could not accept. I knew it was part of my job to understand why these experiences were so bizarre and how they could be seen for what they were - wake-up calls.

Behind all the work I do there is a common thread. That is to help people understand the commonality of this evolution. It happens in many different ways, but it is all designed to get people to experience their full potential as human beings. So I dared to go there bit by bit; I would tell people of my experiences, and if they thought I was mad that was up to them. I quickly learnt not to justify myself, just to express what I knew. After this I had many people contact me because they wanted to talk to someone who would not think that they were mad.

Chapter 71
DNA

Life as we know it to be through our human body consists of science, evolution and religion (which is known as belief). I know life to be made up of three fundamentals as well.

Science is the understanding of the material world and its components, through logical deduction. Evolution is the growth and progression of the planets and all the species that inhabit them, permanently growing and changing. Essence is the spark that allows any of life to happen or form. It is existence.

So the first thing that we need to know is that there is a trinity of all life within any form. Ours as a human being is made up of a mind, body and a soul. A mind with which to discover and deduct, a body that can experience and communicate, and a soul that allows it to happen. So there is a self (body), an understanding of self (mind) and an observing of self (soul).

To get to know our truth we have to embrace all three aspects of self. We are here to discover the nature of the self, within the context of the planet Earth. The trinity (mind/body/soul) is everywhere. There is nothing within this reality that is separate from it. We, and everything around us on this planet, are made of the same components and structures and glue that bind it all together (space). When you become aware of your essence, you discover that there are many different ways of being or not being, as the case may be. This depends on the reality within which you find your essence. But an aspect of us is here on Earth, so whatever we learn is to assist us on this journey through Earth.

The discoveries that we make with our sixth sense are part of a much bigger picture, and we can connect to this picture to see where we are in the scheme of things and to assist us on this journey. It is like a map or a directory. When you tell people about the bigger picture you have discovered, some will believe you, some will think that you are mad, and most will believe that it is your mind playing tricks on you. Becoming aware of the bigger picture, or should I say connecting to your essence, is not done with mind and is not felt through the normal senses that we are used to using. It is so different, and it is the difference that makes you pay attention to the experience. It is received through all of our being (mind/body/soul), but it is not attached to any one aspect. It is only when we try to categorize or understand what it is that we then make it part of our 'human beingness'. When you are in your essence, you know what it is and that it is nothing that is known on an Earthly level. You also know it - in fact you know it far more than you know yourself on a physical Earth level, for you know it to be you, you in your truth. So connecting to your truth is the removal of the illusion, and this removal continues to happen, revealing more and more of the bigger picture to you, of you.

There are many layers that make up the human being, just as there are in an onion, a cabbage or the planet Earth. Each of these layers has its own truth, and it releases it at a moment in our journey, and these moments are there by design; they are part of our blueprint. They are released on instructions from our DNA. They are part of us.

Our DNA contains all the information about us and the journey we are on, even when we will die, and what we will connect to and experience. By this I don't mean information such as you going to the shop or dating a certain person. The information is more about major changes, such as when you will walk, talk, run, turn into a teenager, mature, or die. Also, there is information about diseases that we will experience, whether physical, mental or emotional. But when we learn something that we are here to learn, there is a release mechanism that allows us to move on to the next stage of our journey. So if you are stagnating, or stuck in Groundhog Day, it is because you are not learning what you needed to learn for your own growth. Once you have learnt it, you will move on to your next level. The release mechanism is a form of connecting to your essence - it will make you feel buoyant and alive.

If we reach the stage where we learn through science to read all the information within our DNA, then we will know a great deal more about our journey and ourselves. We can also reach a level through our essence where we can discover our truth about our journey and our self.

The part that is not stored in our DNA is free will, which is our choice. This choice is freedom to be, discover and believe what, how and why.

So the reason why I am writing this book is that within my DNA there was a release that happened, which changed the way I saw or knew life. Then my free will chose to continue this new way of being. And through this I found my journey, within which was the book. Now if I, with my free will, chose to ignore this event that happened, what would my life have been like? It would have had exactly the same outcome, only there would have been more of a battle to get there, and it would have taken a lot longer.

Okay! YOU don't like this thought that you are going to do what you came to do anyway. The reason you don't like it is because you think that you have no control over your own life or future. I told you at the beginning of the book that this is a movie and that we are all playing a part in it. So the book was written and we create the movie. How we play that role is up to us - we can be a positive character or a negative one. Remember, we create the type of personality we are too, and believe me, it takes a long time to create a personality. You may also be forgetting that it is your essence that wrote the book in the first place, so it is only you, creating you, controlling events in your life.

So when we reach this stage on our journey when we realize that there seems to be no point to life, it is already mapped out for us. This is when another level of our being is present. For if it wasn't, we would give up. Not that we can give up. If you think that suicide is giving up then you are wrong. I will cover this topic in a later chapter. This next level gives you the bigger picture, and once you have found it the journey changes, and it is no longer important to you whether life is planned or not, for you are too busy and far too happy discovering the new you in each moment. So within your DNA there are links which allow release at certain times (remembering that there is no such thing as time). The releases happen because of learning. In other words, when you have learnt something, it is registered by your being and this is a signal to your DNA (blueprint) and you move on to the next stage of being you. So although it is set up to happen within a certain time frame, it is really down to you and how long you take to learn. A quick example - look at two baby boys born on the same day and at the same time to twin sisters. These babies will learn to crawl, walk, talk, run at different times, owing to their blueprint and their learning. Now sometimes we spend a long time learning and at other times we spend only a moment. Unfortunately, we say that speed of learning is a great advantage, but there is no difference. We all are here to learn our own truth at our own pace; it will unfold through our learning when we are ready.

The pleasure and the greatness are exactly the same. For example, a Down's syndrome person learning to read is no different from the scientist discovering DNA. Pleasure, achievement, pain and happiness are registered in the same way by everyone, but the way people respond is different. Learning is our motor; it is what keeps us growing and moving. So learn.

Personally, I was learning too much too quickly. I hardly had time to breathe because I was learning on so many different levels, all at the same time. It got quite confusing at times, but when I conquered it the sense of achievement was worth all the effort. The most amazing thing was that there was so much to learn. It was not Earthly book learning that I found so impressive but metaphysical learning. There was so much of it, but all of it came down to the same thing - love. I was studying love and discovering that I was the subject; I was love.

Chapter 72

Dramas

Life sometimes gets the better of you. But you are following your dreams and life should be great if this is true. But you have reached a stage where you are so caught up in the dramas that you have created, or allowed other people to create, that you forget this. When you cannot see beyond or through these dramas, the world and everything in it seems such a dark and heavy place. This is a moment in life that is there by design; it is there so you will reach that point of despair, and go beyond it.

Once you have taken that giant leap of faith and discovered your essence again, you then have to bring that into your physical Earthly reality. There are times when what we create for ourselves is too much, far too demanding, or not even part of the reason we are here. All of our dreams and wishes are a driving force, and part of our essence. Sometimes we get confused and misinterpret our wishes or dreams and the reason and lessons behind them. So when we are caught up in life's dramas, these heavy moments in time, we need to reassess what we truly require. To do this, you need to look at what is going on and why the things that are making you mad, frustrated or sad are happening. If you are doing or living what you believed was your dream, why is it not working? You need to ask yourself what it was you really wanted - were you doing it to prove your worth, or was it was another person's dream that you were caught up in and made your own?

In order to reassess the picture you are in, you need to go beyond it and do this properly (observing). You are then free to see the truth and make new decisions about your life. If you reach this stage and know what you require and then don't put it into action, you will be right back where you started, caught up in the dramas of your life. If, on the other hand, you change the picture to meet your needs and to comply with your own dreams, life then belongs to you. You are in charge of your dramas and your response to them. This does not mean that you control all the events and the people around you. It means that you are in control and able to live your life the way you would like to. So the way you will now react to your dramas is to take action, which is being in control of your reaction and turning it into an action. Now you can move on. You must not wallow in the dramas; you deal with them and free yourself from them. As I said earlier, getting caught up in your dramas happens by design. As you progress on your journey, you will look back and see that design and the perfect way your life unfolds and how silly you were to stand still within those dramas that were just a moment in time that you could have turned into a lifetime.

Dramas are situations you find yourself in. They can be good, bad or indifferent. They are a complete movie show on their own. The reason that they exist is because we get caught up in a moment, attach ourselves to the emotion we feel and hang on to it. We also feed it, by talking and thinking about it, so it gets bigger and bigger, blown out of all proportion. We place too much importance on it and don't let it, or ourselves, move on.

So once you have learnt what dramas really are, you will then learn to free yourself from them.

Chapter 73

Right or Wrong Way

There is not a right way or a wrong way to live or behave, but there is a way, and that way is as individual as we all are. So the correct way to live and be is our way, being true to ourselves. You can only live your truth by knowing it, so what is stopping you?

I have heard so many different reasons why people cannot live their truth, and most of them I have addressed in this modest volume. As previously stated, a major problem that most people come across is that they think that they are living their truth. Indeed they are. But as long as all they see, or know themselves as, is a separate human identity, then it is hard for them to take on board that there is more to them than what they already know. If they are happy being who they are, no matter whether it is the whole truth or not, then where is the harm in that? There is nothing wrong with this at the time; all I am saying is that they will reach a moment in their lives when it does matter. The reason why this will happen is that the Earth and all its inhabitants are evolving into the next stage of being. Just like any discovery that is made on this planet, this takes time to be accepted. So although it might sound or look as if I am telling you the right way to live, I am not. I am giving you reasons or answers to questions that you might have at this moment and trying to explain why we are who we are, in the simplest terms.

To do the kind of work I do is quite hard, because I do not want to put ideas into people's minds and have them believe me. I answer questions that they have through the experiences I have had. This works well for me now. Everything that I now know (essence knowledge) has fallen into place; life makes sense to me. If what I have learnt and know can assist any other being in their journey through life then I am very happy. But I am no dictator. I found a way to be that is right for me. A lot of other people have found that it works for them too. You will do what you need to do for you, and that is great.

160

Chapter 74

The Moment

All our five physical senses are subject to a time delay. This happens because information has to be processed by our brain for us to understand what we are receiving. The speed at which this happens, however, is immense, and we are not aware of the process, until we experience our other senses - the intuitive senses or sixth sense, as it is known. This intuitive information is not received from the physical world and is not passed on to the brain to understand. For once it is there, within the brain's field of energy, we try to make sense of the information and slot it into a box. Yes, you receive the information in the brain, but it is not from the brain. It is so fast that it is overwhelming. People say things such as 'It came from somewhere else', 'That was out of the blue' or 'I don't know where that came from, but it was not from me'. This information is always there, it does not come from anywhere, it is always available; all you have to do is open yourself up to it. The access code to this information is written in your DNA; what you are designed to know you will, one way or another. Just because another person is able to receive certain information does not mean that you will. Everyone is different, and the reason you are here is to experience life as an individual, which you do. Some people have to work on their physical self more than others do; some people connect and then work on themselves. Then there are others who are ready to connect but just need assistance. There is no hard and fast rule. There is always information there for you, but if you want it to be delivered in a certain way or the information to be the same as for so-and-so, then you will miss your truth.

Your connection to yourself is as special as for any other human being. Some may have more people to help and bigger jobs to do. But when you connect to yourself and live your truth, then you will be as happy as all the other people who know their truth. The reason you will be so happy is because you are doing what you came here to do. If you are connecting to your essence and still feeling unhappy, then you have a lot more work to do. This does not mean, however, that when you are living your truth there is no work to do. You are always growing and changing; there is never a point where you stop. And there are always moments of unhappiness, but they do not last for long and they are never of the same intensity as they were. So, whatever it was that triggered me to connect to myself, it is going to be different for you. It normally happens when you least expect it. At that moment there is no expectation, and it is expectation that is the main reason why most people do not connect. For me, it was a haircut that started the ball rolling. Was it the haircut? Was it the anger? Was it the letting go of the anger? Was it because it was my thirty-seventh birthday? No, it was my moment that was not expected.

So what is the moment? It is when time stands still and there is a sense of freedom, freedom from you in your physical form. Within this moment there seems to be a lifetime of time (although there is no such thing as time). This is when you will understand what time is and what it is not. You also have a sense that you really know this moment. It is not strange; it is a truth that you have always known. It is one of the most exhilarating experiences we will ever have, in our human form. You may experience these moments in different situations or intensities. The further along your journey you are, the higher the level you will enter, which will blow anything you have experienced before out of the water. These moments will continue to happen and lift you higher and higher.

The only way we can ever truly feel or know what anything is about is by experiencing it for ourselves. I only wish I could wave a magic wand and have everyone know what their moment is.

Chapter 75
Suicide

I had to come back many times to try to write this passage because every time I thought about it, nothing would enter my head. I think that my personal beliefs were interfering with what might come through. I have since discovered that there is a truth to suicide that was hard to take on board. So I let go and, hey presto, here it is.

As human beings this is an act that we are uncomfortable with. We may, as individuals, have been close to suicide at times. We can think that life is not worth living, but that's as far as we would go. Even now I find it hard to write what I am about to because it goes against what I am and what I feel as Sonya the human being.

Suicide is a lesson on many levels and a lesson for all of us. It is probably viewed as the easy way out, which it is on this level of our awareness. But within another level it is the hardest thing we could ever learn. It is a state of limbo that manifests itself as a continuous circle of recurring experiences. This can only stop when the individual chooses to face their worst nightmare, which made them contemplate the act in the first place. This is living with their self. Once they are able to do this, they will evolve to the next level. The only time suicide makes sense is when viewed from the bigger picture; from this place suicide is about learning and growing.

For all you people out there like me who still think that it is wrong; you are right. It is wrong for you; it is not part of your learning. The people who really hurt are the ones left behind as they are obviously going to find it hard to come to terms with the fact that a loved one did not love them enough to stay. Please remember that this is not about you. Although it is affecting you, it might help you on your journey to assist other people who have suffered in the same way as you.

Death is hard for us to accept, but it is the one sure thing that is going to happen to all of us. Through my experiences, I see death entirely differently. I have experienced the sensation of death. I felt as if I was having a heart attack; my whole body felt as if it was in a vice, and I was scared. The pain got so strong that I felt it was killing me. The only thing I could do was bear it. This was when I accepted it and let go. I no longer wanted to live with this pain. Once I let go, I felt the most amazing sensation I have ever had; I was free, freer than I had thought possible. This was not a heart attack. I was not ill but I left my body the way we do when we die. My out-of-body experience changed my attitude to death.

This chapter is hard to write because I do not want you to think I am promoting death over life. They are both unique and both necessary. We are here to experience both; how we experience them is written into our contract.

I discovered much more about suicide from my clients, those who had experienced it first hand. Mostly, however, I discovered what I know from the higher part of my being. The information was received by me as if I was communicating with the dead person. This is known as mediumship. This does happen and it is real, but it is only real on a certain level of awareness. The information you receive is coming from your higher self, but when we differentiate this information it appears to be an individual energy. The person who is receiving the information from me would know this energy to be the person who has passed on. It is coming from the horse's mouth, so to speak. The dead person no longer exists in the way that we think of existence, but the energy that allowed that person the opportunity to be a human being does exist, just not in an individual format. When I work with mediums who have spent their life doing this work, they may at first disagree with what I say. They are aware that there is far more beyond what they work with and see. They are aware that there is a uniting of energy and that there are many different levels and dimensions to existence. Just like looking at a body with clothes on, then seeing the body undressed, then seeing the body when the skin is removed, until you look at a body through a microscope and discover cells, so there is always more until we reach the point of nothing, and that is the point of existence. Nothing is the ultimate truth. I am not saying here that there is nothing that is the truth. I am saying that nothing, which is beyond definition, is the ultimate truth behind everything that has any form of definition. This is hard for us to comprehend in our individual understanding, and is only knowable through the process of removing everything we know ourselves to be, including our soul essence.

Chapter 76

Soul, Essence, Spirit, Nothing

I think I must try to explain what I mean when I say soul, essence, nothing and spirit. It might help you to understand more.

We have a body that is made of matter, water and space, and it is because of these components that we have a density and a format, a solid appearance. If we were to remove the space, we would be a mere fraction of the size we are, and if we removed the water we would be just particles of dust.

By combining the three, we appear to be a solid lump of reality ('appear to be' being the operative words).

Our soul is a container that is much bigger than our physical body, but it does not contain water, so it is more like dust and space. It is lightweight and has no definite outline. It can expand and contract, it can appear and disappear into the space it is. I cannot describe the soul's size, for this is always changing; it changes with the thought it appears within.

The spirit is the thought or the mind of the soul, the soul being the vessel, the spirit being the driver. The spirit has no format, it is the creative thought.

The essence is the point or the moment before the spirit, so the essence is the power. This power is greater than all and is all. The power is the essence, the soul, the spirit, the human being and the planet that the human lives on, even the sky it looks out at. The essence is everything that exists, including space-time and all matter beyond. All that is and could ever be, is the essence.

The essence comes from nothing, but this nothing is unconditional love in it's purest form; that is because it has no form at all. This love is before essence. This love is the thinker and the thought that creates the thinker. Essence is the thought and spirit is the thought in motion.

Soul is a captured thought and the human is the living reality of that thought.

So, the physical body is the most solid format of a thought that is condensed and known as reality. But the ultimate truth is nothing. But to know nothing is to know all that is. It is also being free from even knowing. To become nothing is the journey of being in any format, and it is nothing that is the secret behind, within and beyond everything.

It is this nothing that we as something cannot comprehend. Once you have experienced that you are more than a body, you discover you are free and you can travel with your soul and discover your spirit. Then you find your essence, or more accurately the essence of everything. You discover that you are everything in existence, and as you grow and learn more, you discover that anything that exists is not the truth. So then you discover, only for a moment, what it is to be before the existence of everything, which is nothing, but you cannot know it while you are in it because there is nothing there to know. (Not even knowing, because thought is a format.) Once you are not in that moment, you can know what it is only because you are the opposite of it. The complete opposite of the secret truth is being a separate identity, which is what we know ourselves to be. And by being this we can discover the secret. So the point of existence is to exist, discover, grow and learn. The truth is the absolute opposite of the reality we know.

The reason we are here is to discover the truth. Once we have discovered the truth, we realize that we are the truth that became something from nothing. So by being the human being, we are the most amazing achievement that sprang from nothing, as well as being that nothing, not that there is anything that can be in nothing. Without this body, mind, matter, spirit, soul, essence, we could not discover the ultimate truth.

So, as individual beings, we are the most important part of existence, for we are existence. And only by being this are we able to discover before this and after this. This means we have the ability to know, and knowing is pure wisdom, and this is our access to the truth.

Chapter 77
Comfort

To move forward in our life we have a great need to feel comfortable. This comfort we find in many ways and many different things, such as a warm jacket or a soft warm bed, nice food that makes us feel good, a loving relationship, shoes that don't hurt, being comfortable with the way we look or what we have to say.

So, when you find yourself looking to be comfortable, you are more than likely in for a change, and this change will depend where you are on your journey. You are protecting yourself from life in order to dare to go there, wherever there is. This is a stage that allows you to grow spiritually. It is the security that you are really looking for, within the comfort that you seek. But it is the moving forward and taking risks that end up giving you strength and the security you seek. It is an inner security that you discover by taking a chance on life, not a false security, which is the one we use with our materialism. Don't get me wrong; there is nothing wrong with creating a warm, loving place to be. This is great. It is when you use it to hide or when you are in desperate need of comfort that life is about to change. Security is who you are, not what you think you are. And believe me, there is a very big difference between who and what. Your comfort zone is a place for your Earthly body, but it is not required for your essence, which is what you truly are.

Chapter 78
Security

Security is a way of feeling or a means of being secure. The society that we live in today is all about the latter. We find security in money, relationships, houses, etc.; it is always based on things outside of us. The truth is that security comes from within; it is a state of being with or without anything else.

Okay, we all need food, shelter and water to feel physically and mentally secure. We also need to give and to receive love to feel emotionally secure. But beyond that, what has happened to us all? We have become so programmed in life that money and power seem to be the only things that give us security. Well, this is a false sense of security, as we all know that money can come and go, in the same way that relationships do.

Feeling secure is one of our greatest needs on all levels - it is essential to our growth. Have you ever noticed when insecure people suddenly come into a large amount of money or into a position of power, they become cocky and rude? For the first time in their lives they feel secure - so secure that they feel they don't need anyone else. This is, of course, simply a false sense of security. It only lasts as long as the money or the position is there, or until they have no true friends or loved ones left. True security comes from within; when you are living your truth you have all the feeling of security you could want.

Of course, life is better and easier if you have more than enough money to cover your basic needs. All the luxuries that we enjoy are great, but they can never really give us a true feeling of being secure. That only comes from living and connecting to your truth, living and being the person you are here to be. We in the West live a very material existence. I am not saying that it is wrong. Materialism is just another form of energy that we interact with. But it is when we make it our god that it becomes a problem. All the money in the world or all the power in the world will only make you feel happy and secure for a moment, and then what?

Being secure is all about feeling safe and protected, but from what? The outside world, other people, Mother Nature, our death, or death in general? We want guarantees, but I am sorry to say there are no guarantees. We are here to experience life, so why would we want to lock ourselves away and not share ourselves with the world? I know that there are people who will take what we think is ours; our husbands, our houses, our money, even our life. Is there anything that we can do about that? Nothing really belongs to us other than our self, and even this is on loan for a period of time.

There are always ways to protect the illusion of what is ours, by teaching people who they truly are. For once you know your truth then you will not have any need to take what appears to belong to another person. We only have the use and enjoyment of anything that is made up of matter. There is only one thing that no one can ever take away from you, and that is your soul; it is the only thing that is really and truly yours. But please remember this only applies whilst you are in your body. For when you no longer have a body, then your soul joins the essence, which is the same essence as the other people who have lived then died. Once you understand this, then you will know that everything in your life is there for a period of time (including your body), so enjoy it all while you have it and learn to let go when it has gone. This is what makes a secure human being.

I believe that we feel insecure when we hold on too tightly to what we believe to be ours. Once we let go, the truth of the situation is revealed. We will have a greater understanding and this will help us to grow. As this separate identity, we learn to create a protection field because we feel all alone. There is no one we can ever trust completely other than ourself. So this need for security comes from our separation. Then, when we discover our truth, we understand why we needed to feel secure and protected. The world out there is full of all kinds of things that could be scary, so the more money we have the bigger garden we can have, along with the bigger fences and electric gates to defend it, and the more we are able to keep out this scary stuff called life.

It is quite funny, when you look at it from a different angle - we are here to live and know what it feels like to be a separate identity. Being secure is when you are happy and content being you. If you have the need to put up protection then you are not free to be yourself. True security comes from really knowing yourself in a physical, mental and, most of all, a spiritual way. And to get to know you, you will have to take time, and make the effort, to discover you.

Chapter 79

Reincarnation

Reincarnation has many different truths; what it is and how it is viewed depends on from where it is being observed. To start with, I will try to explain it from a level that is the highest I am aware of at this moment. From this perspective, there is no such thing as reincarnation. In our terms, reincarnation means to come back to Earth and live again in a new body. At this point of existence you are not only living many different lives all at the same time, in different time frames, but also living many different types of realities in many different locations within the universe. At this high level of existence, our energies join up and we become one essence. For example, at this level there would be everything in existence being everything there is to be, so you would know yourself as being 'all that is'.

When we look at reincarnation from an Earthly point of view, it exists for some people, for they may remember that they were someone else, but the truth is that you are being that person at the same time you are being this one. Remember that it is time that allows us a past, present and a future. When in truth, from an outside higher level/ point of view, time does not exist. There is only the moment, and it is impossible to understand this moment with your five human senses or your logical Earthly mind. But this moment lasts forever, although if I say that, then I am giving it a time frame which it is not part of.

You are reading this book in your now moment, which I am talking to you about. This is in my past moment, as you would know it, but it is in my moment of now, as I am typing it, and I see it in your future moment. What I have just said is all happening at the same moment. Just as in watching a movie and going from one scene to another, you are watching the person on the typewriter and then you flash to another scene where the person is reading the book that is being typed in the other scene. So life is like looking at this giant movie screen with literally millions of scenes all going on at the same moment, all interconnected with each other.

Back to reincarnation. As I said earlier, there are many different truths and they each belong in their own unique reality. So within some of these levels/dimensions/realties, reincarnation does exist because it is within some people's level of awareness. It is part of their laws of truth. So the truth, the whole truth, is only true to where you find your attention to be. If you use your other senses you will be able to uncover many different truths. So, yes, reincarnation does happen, and no, there is no such thing as reincarnation. Confusing, eh? Well, don't worry about it, it will all come out in the wash.

Chapter 80
Our Body

Most people resent their own body; they always want what they don't have. There is another reason why people resent their bodies that is not generally known. That is that it does not represent our truth, our essence. It is impossible for a body to represent us in our truth, for it would be everything and nothing all at the same time, which it is being, but we don't know that this is so. The body is a tool that we have chosen and we continue to choose what it is like in every moment.

What does your body say about you and your life or journey? Is your body your main priority? Is it cared for through nutrition, exercise and sleep? Does your body look and feel alive and healthy? Is your body a good representation of the way you feel or want to feel about life?

Our bodies say many things about our journey and ourselves; but sometimes our assessment of our bodies is a bit cloudy. There are a lot of people who are totally off balance because they pay far too much attention to how they look and forget the mind and the soul. My body has always been my last consideration, until now, that is, as it is playing me up. It obviously has needs that I am not meeting. I was lucky in that my body was quite balanced and basically energetic, but the years of neglect are now taking their toll. I am slightly overweight for my height, and have far too many wrinkles and wobbly bits for my liking. These are the problems on the outside. Inside my body is tired and craves energy, not the energy that is our essence, for I have plenty of that; the energy that comes from the Earth we live on. I have been very busy over the last six years working with my mind and essence, and my body all of a sudden needs attention. It is hard work for me to pay attention to my body, in the same way that it might be hard work for you to pay attention to your mind or your soul.

We are a trinity of being and to be who we truly can be and who we truly are, we need to pay attention to all of us. As for the way we look, that is by design. You are here to discover many different things, and your body is perfect and ready for you to do this. If your body is small and round then you know that you are not here to be a fashion model or to do any job that requires height, so don't waste time pursuing careers that are not made for you. Take a good look at your body and give it what it needs to allow it to be the best it can be. Look at what makes you happy, at your hobbies; could you make a living out of them? Please don't think that when I say if your body is small life is limited, for it isn't. Don't waste time on something unless it is a real passion. Passion is the main driving force in our lives. Sometimes we put necessity first, which, of course, we have to, as long as it is not soul-destroying. Always follow your heart first and then bring your head into the equation. For a really balanced life, you need to use your intuition at all times, for it is the part of you that is in the know.

Chapter 81
Death

Death is moving from one reality into another. On a physical Earth level, all we are aware of, it is the end of a life, a personality, a mother, a father, a friend, a son or a daughter. It is the end of our physical relationship with another human being. It is the most painful experience that the people who are left behind will probably ever go through.

Why do we need to suffer when someone we love dies? Why have they taken a place in our lives that no one else could fill? What could we possibly learn from our loss?

Within our normal sense of the world, there is no sense to it; there seems to be no reason for death at all. Grieving is the only thing that we have. When a person dies, does grieving offer us anything other than pain? Within our loss and suffering there is a truth, which is you, and there are moments when you are closest to your truth. If you fully embrace these moments and do not hide or run from them, they can set you free, free to know your truth. When you are aware of the bigger picture then it all falls into place. We will always have a past with these people, and this is within our memories. They are no longer in our moment but they will be in our future. Death is really a release and a connection at the same moment; it is a release of the physical body and a connection to the energy body. You are moving on, you have achieved great success, and you get to move a step closer to your truth/home. The body is from Earth and it goes back to Earth at some point. We all know that we will die but we refuse to accept this. We spend our lives trying to run from death; we do everything we can to stay alive. The reason we avoid death, even talking about it, is because we fear death. This is only natural, for we see and know it to be the end. But it is only the end to our physical body and the concept of our separate identity.

The way to understand death is with senses other than the five Earthly senses. When we understand death by knowing - not Earthly intellectual knowing, but essence knowing - this is the moment we start living. When we know our truth we learn to embrace life. That is why you are here, to see, smell, taste, feel and hear, as a separate living being. All of these five senses allow you to discover many things and to create many different possibilities and turn them into reality.

The world is here for us to discover and then create. And while we are on this journey, we have the opportunity to discover our secret, and there are many ways to do this. First and foremost, however, we need to discover life. Then we can open ourselves up to death. And it will change the way we feel about it.

I was privileged to be at my grandmother's death, which was a long, slow process. She was ninety-three years old, or ninety-three years young - whichever way you look at it. She was an amazing woman; so gracious right till the end. She had had an experience just before her ninety-third birthday, which I have already mentioned. It was all about going somewhere new, but very familiar. She met lots of people who were dead that she knew, and others who she felt she knew, but not from her Earth life. What she was describing was the same as a lot of people who have had near-death experiences have described. She was also describing feelings and sensations that I have experienced, and she was so happy that I knew what she was talking about.

The night of her death, she was having similar experiences and was living, it seemed, in two worlds at the same time. The energy that was in that room was beautiful. I will never forget the amazing things that happened that night. She taught me what death was and how to accept it, which I already had, but I was now putting this into practice. I miss her dearly, but I feel her more now than when she was alive. It is as if her energy has merged with mine and she is always with me.

The more I learned about death the more I learned how to live life. The time you have, on this planet, in this reality, in this body, is so short. It passes so very quickly. There is so much to experience and enjoy, and it is death that gives us that driving force. Don't put it off, that thing you want to do, take action to make it happen, create and live the life you are here to have. What is stopping you?

Each day I live the person I have discovered myself to be. By doing this I know my true reason for being. I enjoy being me and I would not swap any part of me now, for anything. I could not be anything other than what I am; you could say I am the perfect actress for the part.

Chapter 82
Self-realization

This is the when a person discovers his/her self beyond their human awareness, a step closer to their true nature. To be self-realized is to know you as a physical, mental, emotional and spiritual being. There are many other aspect to you as a being, but self-realization basically consists of knowledge of these four aspects. It is a paradox of being and not being at the same moment.

Within our normal way of knowing, there is only being. But once we discover that there is far more to us than the body and the space we inhabit, it changes the way we see and know life. When we have reached this stage of being, we live life with two different realities that are totally opposite in all of their structures, concepts, natural laws, and energy fields. It is very hard to balance these two totally different realties, for we have only ever been assisted in how to be a human being. So many people feel that they are losing their minds or that their imagination has gone haywire. Most of the time people just ignore what is happening to them (if they can). Self-realization is when a person has managed to balance these two ways of knowing and being, and is able to blend them to become one realized being.

Our bodies and our brains are designed to make us believe that we are simply the result of an evolutionary cellular process which is a human being. The reason for this is so that we can learn everything there is to know about being a restricted, contained, separate identity. With this learning we grow on all levels. When we are being on our soul level, the Earth's issues are not important and seem so simple. This is because of the knowing we have at this observation level. Our essence knows that we have chosen this experience to learn what we are not, and in doing so we will grow through our wisdom into another reality.

Self-realization happens at any time, anywhere, to anyone. There is not one particular thing that you can do, nor a test that you can sit. For it will happen when it is going to and that is when you choose it to happen. But the choosing is not just saying to yourself, 'Okay, now.' It is letting go and being, and that is what people don't know how to do. It is written into your script, so your DNA (blueprint) will contain information about when you will get to know your truth. It is not attached to time, only learning. So by letting go you are making a choice to follow your contract. At the point of letting go you become self-realized.

I know that what I am saying suggest that there is no point in actively doing anything in life to discover your truth. But there is a great deal of understanding that is required to make it easier for you on your journey to yourself. That is why I am bothering to sit here and type when I really don't like typing!

How this happens to us is a mystery, but one thing is certain - the only thing we have to do is be. Yes, that is it, just be! The problem is that when we know that there is more to life, we have a great need to do something to get there. So by trying to be, you are not being. By specifying what to do in order to be, you are defining being, and this is not being. So being is being fully present within the moment of now and not having any expectation or description or requirements, quieting the mind, by not trying to. If you try and it does not work, pay attention to a thought but don't try to get rid of it. You will connect, but it will just happen, and once it has, you will want to stay in that place forever, although you will not know how to maintain the connection at first. You will lose it because you will try to hold on to it or become desperate and infuriated with yourself, which will have the opposite effect to what you want. So please note what I have to say, as it will help you to embrace your different levels of being as one.

Self-realization is the moment when life makes sense.

Self-realization is the moment when you find yourself free.

Self-realization is where miracles happen.

Self-realization is part of the bigger picture.

Self-realization is when you learn how perfect you are and have always been.

Self-realization is knowing and observing yourself, as a self and beyond.

I could go on and on, for there is no real way to explain the truth; you can only know it. There is nothing that we know within our planet, however great, that even comes close to the truth. All I have to work with is these words.

This journey that I am on is so rewarding. It is the small, simple truths that I come across that impress me the most. Whatever I do or say has meaning, and the meaning it possesses is magical and uplifting. I don't know how I used to live and be happy without this truth. I really did not know that there was something missing until I found it. I am in awe of myself, not as a physical being but as an essence that is 'all that is'.

Chapter 83
Changes

Everything changes in a moment; each moment is contained within a fraction of time that is not measurable; each moment is new and has never been before. Are we fully aware of these facts? Well, given the way we live on this planet, you would not think so. Each moment is not only new but each moment is full of possibility and probability. What each moment turns into is up to us. Yes, we all have the power and ability to choose our moments. There are many people and events going on all around us all of the time. Our secret power lies in how we choose to respond or how we choose to feel, think and be. You cannot interfere with other people's choice of how they spend their moments, but you most certainly can choose yours. For example: it is you who is choosing to read what I am typing, and I have no say in that. It is me who is choosing to type these words, and you have no say in those. Most of the time we believe that we do not have a choice, and if this is true it means that there is no moment. If there is no moment, then there is no reality. Once you discover the magical secret within a moment, you also discover non-reality, space, 'all that is', and the truth of you.

The gap in between is where it all truly is. Yes, maybe you have got it! The moment is all there truly is, and it is your thought that turns that moment into whatever you require it to be. That moment is where all the enlightenment, all the self and self-realization are. All the existence and non-existence you could possibly imagine, all is in that moment. So by choosing your moment you are creating your own reality, and also freeing yourself from it.

However old you are, think of all the moments that you have already lived through, that you have missed, and all the moments in your future that you might miss. Each moment changes everything, and the reason we do not take these moments is because we like to feel real and solid and structured, in order to know that we exist. That is why we have a body, to allow us the pleasure of knowing ourselves as a real separate entity.

Believe me, you will not spend the rest of your life in the moment. For if you did, then you would not be a physical being. You would be an aspect of being and not being at the same moment, and would have no reason to do or be, for you would always not be. So we choose a body to be able to do the many other wonderful things which all fall into the category of doing.

Okay, back to change. Now each moment is new and it is up to us what we do with that moment. Our biggest problem is that we always project who we are by living in a moment of the past. We thus limit our full potential and all the probabilities that are there for us to discover. Remember, we live in the past to feel real and separate. Illness and addiction sit within these past living moments. The cellular structure of our body is programmed by our conditioned mindset, which we have learned. Healing can have a drastic effect by removing the mindset of your cellular memory.

Before you all jump on my back, there are many illnesses that are there for us to learn, and, of course, we all need a way out of our physical life. Healing still works in this type of situation ,but more in a form of acceptance of death or suffering which makes life easier to live.

I know that we never want to take full responsibility for ourselves, but if we don't, who else will? Also, remember that when you were writing your movie, before you came into physical reality, you may have wanted to know what it really felt like to be ill or addicted. When you are not aware of there being more to you than your normal humanness, you will never take anything I am saying on board. It's not because you don't want to, but because you cannot. For in your own unique contract you needed to know the totality of what it means to be a human being. But if you managed to find yourself within a moment of now, then you would understand yourself and your illness or addictions.

There is something I want you to know about your movie. You chose your part but it was also designed to accommodate the movie of every other being on this planet throughout the whole of existence. So the part you are aware of playing, at this moment, is a small part in the movie called the universe. Now have you ever seen one of those movies or plays where there is only one person playing every role throughout?

This is your role too, only it is not just clothes and make-up that change you, it is bodies, time, space and all matter. You also have to play planets, space, time and even the universe. The day I discovered this was the day I saw the newness of life, how everything in this universe is changing all the time and how I kept it in one place, to allow me to exist the way I thought I was. I could only measure myself (to know myself) against something that was constant and static. Everything had to be solid and real for me to exist.

We are all creatures of habit and all of these habits are a part of the person we know ourselves to be. The reason that we are habitual is that it is our custom and our human nature - a familiarity that makes us feel so real, so that we belong to this world. There are habits that are bad for our physical well-being and there are other habits that are detrimental to our essence/soul. If you believe that you don't have any habits, think of what you do every day that is the same, done in the same way, for most of your life. Even the way you think is habitual. For us to change it feels like going against ourself, which we are; by not defining who we think we are, we free ourself from ourself.

Chapter 84

Discovering You

When we are small children, we are full to the brim of possibilities and probabilities. This is called full potential. As we start to grow, we discover our limits; these in turn have an effect on the type of person we are going to be. Some of those limits are down to our age and stage of being. As we grow we have the opportunity to try them again, and to our amazement we may well discover that we can now do what we thought we couldn't. Unfortunately, some people never get the opportunity, or simply don't bother to try again, and this will give a structure to their abilities that is probably incorrect. They saw themselves as limited.

For example, when you were a small child your teacher told you that you would never make an artist, so you believed her and never bothered to try all the different art mediums that exist. You grew up believing that you were not creative. Then one day, someone asks you to help them out at a local fair, painting children's faces, making them into clowns. You naturally say, 'I'm no artist,' and she says, 'You don't need to be, it's easy.' So you do this for your friend. And guess what? You are so good at it that you end up making a career out of your new-found artistic talent.

School is one of the main places where we learn what we are capable of achieving, but most happy, successful, talented people did not discover who and what they were capable of at school. I would have been great at psychology or philosophy, but the opportunity was not presented to me at my school. And at that stage on my journey, I would not have responded in the same way that I do now.

To discover our journey we first need to discover ourselves. So you think that you know who and what you are? Think again! By now this book must have told you something about life that you had not considered before. What happens to us all is that we reach a point in life when we think that we know who we are, and then something happens that wakes us up, and, I might add, not by accident. Then we realize that maybe there is more to us than we thought there was, and this is the start of the discovery of you. You may think that you know yourself as a human being but there is so much more for you to discover about your essence and your soul, which you could spend a lifetime discovering. This is what we are here for and what you will do. Discovering your truth changes everything, even the person you thought you knew.

We owe it to ourselves to discover what we are capable of doing and being. There is never just one thing that we are here to do; there are countless ways to learn and to experience.

First we must discover the world through our five senses. Each of these senses allows us to connect to the world around us and allows it to connect to us. To ignore the world around us is to ignore what the world has to show, tell and share with us.

There are so many people who are not being true to themselves. They are pretending to be someone they would like to be, or following a fashion trend. As children we can discover how to be in with the in-crowd. As adults we need to follow our own journey, which can be scary at times, but it is worth it.

The biggest problem that people have is when they are not being true to themselves. Most people do not know what I mean by being true to yourself. It means honouring the person you are and the person you are going to be in each new moment, and freeing yourself from a description that restricts your growth. Avoid putting yourself in a mould; free your potential and discover just how incredible you are. It is part of our journey to discover as much as we can about ourselves, the world we live in and beyond. There are many clues to help us to fulfil our contract. There is passion - the things in life that ignite your spark. They are talking to you. Think about the people you enjoy being with and why, or what it is that you enjoy about being with them. You may think they are good company, but there are always so many levels at work at the same time. The true reason you know and like each other might appear out of the blue one day.

But all of this is a waste of time if all you do is go to work for money, go to bed for sleep and watch TV or go to the pub for something to do. You have to put yourself out there to discover what makes you feel great. And I mean on all levels - mentally, emotionally, physically and spiritually. You are here to grow and learn, not sit back and accept that you know who you are. You have a lifetime of learning and living to do. You owe it to yourself.

By writing this book, I am living a part of my contract. I am also being a mother, a lover and wife to my husband, a friend, teacher, student, and I travel to many different countries and interact with many different people. I know that I am on this planet for many different reasons and each is important in its own right. But all of it is what I am here for, so I do not intend to leave any of it out.

Chapter 85
Infill

As you will have gathered by now, I am talking about you and the discovery of the you that you have yet to know. I am talking about not taking yourself and others for granted. I am talking about your limitations; everything that you know yourself to be is in the past. Once you learn to live in more of your moments, then your life and world expand beyond your wildest dreams.

There are many things in my life now that are there because I allowed myself the freedom to be. It all came about because I changed my attitude to life, because of an experience that was beyond my control. Control is what stops us from being free. We will always be in control of our true self, but trying to control is detrimental to our truth. The way I now live has not changed a great deal in appearance. This is down to the fact that I was living my life pretty close to my contract anyway. Your life might change drastically once you discover more and more of your truth. But it is not the change that is so impressive; it is the way you see and understand life that knocks your socks off.

My best description for my life now is that there is far more of me, Sonya, living my life. There is much more of me experiencing, enjoying and learning. The only thing that was missing from my life before (not that I felt there was anything missing until I started to discover it) was me, myself and I. Now I am fully present and accounted for and taking full responsibility for my journey and loving every minute of it, the highs and the lows (yes, I do have them!).

Chapter 86
Choice and Choosing

To choose is to use your free will. To choose is an amazing ability. What most people don't recognize or acknowledge fully is that it is the choosing that creates their life. We all know this is fact but we don't realize how powerful the choices that we make are. People stagnate when they don't make the right choices for themselves. I was going to say when they don't choose, but they are choosing not to choose, which, of course, is a choice. So, whatever is not working in your life is because you are choosing it. I know that things happen that we do not choose, but how we respond is the choice that we have the right to make. People have said to me that the time is not right yet for them to choose. It is not right because they are choosing for it not to be right. It is choosing it to be the right time that makes it the right time, and the same thing that was going to happen in the future will happen in the now moment.

So what they are truly saying is that they are choosing not to be ready to handle the situation at this moment. This is fine, but the outcome is going to be the same, whenever it is that they choose to take action. When you have made a choice and it is not working for you, then you need to discover if it is teaching you something that you need to learn, or if is it simply not for you. If so, choose again. So many people make a choice in their life and stick with it, even when it proves to be a bad choice. Why? If it is not for you, then make another choice.

Thinking is the starting process in your life; choosing is the thought you are going to go along with; and action is putting that thought and choice out there. Creation complete. You must also realize that you choose the thought before you think it. So when a thought enters your head, where did it come from? You. There are thoughts that appear out of the blue, which are universal or intuitive, but you choose to listen and tune in to them. You also choose what you do with them. (Not forgetting that they are the bigger part of you.) Most of the time, when we tune in to universal thought waves, we dismiss them or label them as our own thoughts (which they are in essence). The reason is that we find it hard to know the difference. I believe that when we feel free to speak our mind, this is when we free our intuitiveness. By speaking our truth we honour our self and those around us. But to be able to be free to speak our mind we have to feel that we are being fair and true. To do this we need to see the bigger picture. And to see the bigger picture you need to be true to yourself! (I know - another Catch-22). So, as you can see, when journeying to our self, we always reach Catch-22 situations. The only way out of it is not to look at it with our normal thinking process, but to observe it from a distance. There you will find the answer to your Catch-22. Once you observe from a distance, then you have removed your mind from the concept and containment of your brain and set it free. This is freeing yourself or, should I say, your essence to be able to play the role it is designed to. Normally there is an event in your life that takes you to this freedom of being. The event can come about in many different ways. Whatever way it is activated, you will know it when it happens.

Chapter 87
The Start of You

On this journey of discovery that we are all on, we reach a point that is our truth. This truth is called many things but I will call it enlightenment. It is the part of your journey where the light, which is you, is present. This, however, is the starting point, not the conclusion, of your journey. Once you discover who you truly are, you then have to live this truth through your human body, and this can be the hard part. It would be easy if every other being on the planet were at the same point as you, but they are not. Unfortunately, we affect each other in either a good way or a bad way (cause and effect). This is because in truth there is no such thing as separation.

Once we have found our light, then we have to shine it for the world to see. Enlightenment is not the goal or the end of the road; it is the start of an amazing journey.

Chapter 88
Good and Evil, God and Devil

The creative essence energy is what we would call good or God. The opposite of this creative energy is stagnation, which is what we would call evil or the Devil. In truth, energy is pure potential, and it is our use of that energy that is positive or negative, or what we would call God or Devil. We use this energy for life; living, killing, destroying - the choice is ours. The reason why we use energy as we do is that we know ourselves as separate. The truth is that you are that energy, so you are good and evil.

So on this planet of separation, we have every opportunity to discover the truth, whether we use a positive or a negative way. But once we have discovered this energy, then the only way we can live is in a balanced, positive way. Not because we are forced to but, because we discover the truth that there is no separation, it would be pointless harming ourself. Murderers, rapists, any people we regard as evil have the same essence within them as saints, Jesus, Buddha, you and me. It is their ignorance or their non-discovery of the truth which allows them not to be responsible for their actions. For remember, it is not who they are, it is what they do that we call evil.

Then where do you draw the line at killing? Is it okay to kill for religion or to protect a belief or a principle, even a country? We so freely throw stones at one type of destruction and cheer on another. And when we sit and take a look at what we find acceptable, we justify it is as okay.

Think again!

The world is changing, and if we help other people to discover their truth, then the world will automatically be a more positive, balanced place. There will always be opposites on this planet, for it is a place of learning. We discover our truth by having an opposite-polarity planet. What is missing is the balance, which is the equator, the middle ground and the ability to be positive or negative. This is all one needs. When we are free to be whatever we require, we feel more alive than if we were forced to choose. We often find it quite difficult to live with the people we love, let alone people from another country. Why is it so hard for us to live together? Because we sometimes live a life that is not the life we want. But instead of doing something about it, we just moan and fight. Living the life that you are here to live makes you a free being. But most people want others to live their way too. And this will never work.

Think about all the problems that you have with the people in your life. I bet that all the arguments you have are because they want to do something different from what you want to do. You may think that if we all start doing what we want to, then no one would live together. Have you seen how many single moms there are in the world? The world is not working very well the way it is now. The alternative I am advocating is a place for all of us and a role to play, and the sooner we start playing that role then the world will work the way we (we being 'all that is') designed it to be. Not that it could ever be anything other than what it is.

Here I go again!

I do what I do because of you and you do what you do to allow me to do what I do. I could go on and on but the point I am trying to make is that without each other we have no role to play. So I could not be a writer if there was no one like you to read my book. It is my role to write and yours to read, and that is by design. But if you did not have the ability to read then I would not have the ability to write. One thing creates the other. One is no greater than the other but each exists because of the other.

This next passage is closer to the truth because it is part of the bigger picture. You are going to have a real hard time with what I have to say unless you, yourself, can know the bigger picture. So please forgive me if you find this offensive, but I cannot describe the truth if I don't write this. We are here to discover what it is like to be a separate, living, feeling, seeing, tasting and hearing human. Now to be able to experience everything that these senses have to offer us, and to truly know ourself as a self, we require many different things. Some things will happen to us and some things we will cause by our actions. If these events do not happen, then we will not have the experience that comes with them, which we are here to know.

So, as far as the bigger picture is concerned, there is no such thing as good or bad; there is only learning, which is growth. This paragraph makes a mockery of the one that came earlier but that is because this paragraph is part of the bigger picture, not the Earthly reality we find ourselves in. This will make more sense to you as we progress further. But please remember that it is our perception that governs our truth. And if you are observing life from one perspective, then that will be its truth. When your observation point changes, then so does the truth.

When I told certain people about my psychic abilities, they said that it was the Devil working through me. This obviously scared me and forced me to do some real in-depth soul-searching. I knew I was a naturally good person, if there is such a thing. I had always been interested in helping and being kind. After a while, I realized that it was their fear of the unknown and their lack of personal experience that were fuelling their attack on my experiences. My doubt was constructive but painful. I even decided to ignore what was happening to me at one point, but life then became mundane. I was living like a robot, as I used to, except I was unaware of this at the time. Through that experience I learnt that I should not care about the opinion of others and continue to follow what my life was showing me. This changed everything; I freed myself and I learnt to trust myself.

Chapter 89
Trust

What is it to trust? What does it mean to us? Trust is a major part of humanity; we have a belief system that needs to be maintained. For this belief to exist, we build a wall around ourselves and only let certain people in. So trust is a form of protection from the world, or should I say the people of the world. There are so many different walls that we put in place to protect our way of being. There are our loved ones, to whom we reveal and from whom we require the most trust. Then there is our circle of friends, with whom we share some of our secrets. There is our social circle, which we perform for. There is our town community and our country unity and then our humanity, and all of this needs protecting.

But protecting from what? Why do we feel the need to protect ourselves and only trust certain people?

What happens when we do take people into our confidence? Yes, most of the time they let us down. And why do the people we trust with our innermost feelings betray us? Because it is human nature to share, not hide and protect. It is because we have an innate natural ability to take care and share with our own, and the truth is that every person on this planet is our own. The only time that we would be aware of this is if we were attacked by some other life form, which did not belong to our Earth, or, of course, if we discover our own truth and our connection to the world and everything in it.

We trust and need to trust because we do certain things in our lives that we do not want to share with everyone, for they might judge us, and this is going against our basic nature. So we need to trust to be able to expose our truth. When you reach the point of understanding human nature, and consider the fact that each and every one of us is capable of anything and everything, you realize that most of our problems cause us pain because we don't speak or live our truth. This is because we think and know ourselves to be separate within our own little world that needs to be protected from the rest of those separate worlds. We need to trust someone so we can reveal our self and still be loved. Love is what trust is all about. Only if someone loves us will they not betray us and expose us to the world. Wrong, because the first person that we decide to trust, when we are grown up, is a lover. In the past we would hold on to this relationship, no matter how bad it was, because we sought to protect our truth, even at the cost of forsaking our self. There was probably also the matter of wedding vows. In today's society, we no longer put up and shut up. What happens when you fall out with someone? They expose you, and you find out. The next lover gets less exposure from you and less of you, to prevent it happening again. And so the story goes, until you meet someone who you think is the one and you fully trust again and expose your inner self.

It is laughable really, when all you have to do is be who you are and expose yourself. Then you don't need to trust anyone, for you are not hiding.

We believe we are bad or not normal when, in truth, everyone is the same when it comes down to our core or essence. Remember, you are an essence shining through a soul that has taken on the form of a human body. So the trust that we require is self-trust. We only need to trust ourselves to be the person we are here to be.

It is the illusion of self that needs protecting. Not your truth. After I learned to trust myself, I learned to share myself with the world. I was certainly not going to hide this amazing discovery of life that I'd made. I dared to be, but to do that I had to learn so much. Most of all, I had to learn that I had a right to be and know myself as I chose to be. I could not perform for the world or pretend that I was free, and I knew it. Even at the risk of being persecuted, I dared to be. I know it sounds strange that an English woman in the twenty-first century could be persecuted, but it was bound to happen. I put a stop to it by freeing myself from the opinions of others. Remember, we all have opinions and they are as unique to each of us as the way we look. There is no one way that is right; there is simply our way. It takes time to discover our sense of self, but time is only an illusion that we find ourselves within. Yes, it is time that allows us to be a human being, it is time that gives us birth and death and growth in between. It is time that lets us believe that we are separate and time that allows us to change and learn, and yet this great thing called time is what keeps us from our truth in more ways than we could possibly imagine.

Chapter 90
Clearing the Way

I thought that I would try to clarify our role.

We as human beings are here to learn. In fact we never stop learning. We also learn as a spirit and a soul in a totally different way. Everything that we do on this planet in this body has already happened. Only we are not aware of this as a human being with five senses. This is because we are contained within this happening. It is similar to a movie on a CD - it will always be contained on that CD. Now this being the case, we will only ever do what we have in fact already done. This means that there is nothing in our life that we can change because it is set, in the original movie. Even though we are at this moment creating that movie. It is our dimensional reality of time and space that gives us the illusion that there is a past, present and future; if you remove those division you are left with a moment of now, and that is over just as quickly as I could think of it.

This event called planet Earth (it is an event because it is over) was created by us on many different levels. The thought that created Earth came from our essence, and the reality on Earth from us being present in human form within the thought. We are the living thought. While we are being this thought we have the ability within our minds to discover that what we truly are is that thought. We cannot change that thought but we can discover the magical secret truth of it.

So then I have to ask myself why I am bothering to write these words or help people to change their lives. Because they are going to do what has already happened anyway and there is no way I can change their minds. The answer is that it is written in my CD or my movie; in other words I cannot stop myself even if I wanted to, and if I did stop then this was what I was going to do. This might sound as if it is just a fob-off, but it is the way I know it to be. I am a very happy person and that is because I am aware of this information through my higher conscious knowing, and it is this higher knowing that makes my movie, which is my life, easy.

I will give you an example that I hope will help you to understand more.

Let's say one of these passages in this book is there for you because it is written within your movie that you will read this book. So then it is written within my movie that I will write this book. Some of theses words will have an effect on you, even if you are not aware of it. You are playing your part just by reading this book, and please remember that there was no way that you were not going to read it. What happens to you while you are reading this book will be what is written in your movie. You may like it, you may hate it, this is not the important part; what is important is that you play your role, which is to read it, which you will. Now that might be the case, but it could be that you need to write a letter to me, to tell me that some particular part of the book did not make sense to you. I will read your letter and look into the part you were referring to. Then let's say that in the future your comments caused me to write another book, all about this topic that you did not understand. This in turn will have an effect on you, me and all the other people connected to us. This could all have been part of a process to get me to write another book, so that more people can discover their truth. Or it could all have happened so that you meet the man or woman of your dreams because you bumped into one another at the bookstore and you both had my book in your hands. Or it could be that both of these events are part of our movie. This is synchronicity, the secret magic of life that is all around us, but we generally only pay attention to the major events, not the small stuff that really makes it happen.

What I am saying in these words is for you and they will have an effect, even if it is only in the form of criticism. Never forget that great things can come from the hardest form of criticism.

So we will each play our part for each other to create the whole that already exists.

Chapter 91
Upbringing

We are all a result of our upbringing. How many times have you heard this quote? And how true is it? When we enter a physical body we are an essence that is not sure how to make this body work, for all this body is able to do at that moment is cry, gurgle, urinate, etc. As this body starts to grow, and with the encouragement of our caretakers, it discovers new ways to express itself. Over the next twenty years or thereabouts, these caretakers will help and encourage us to grow the way they believe life requires us to be. They may not be very good at this job, but we mostly reach the next stage. This is the stage when we are on our own. At what age this happens varies for everyone. We are handed the key and it is up to us. Or is it? We have spent however many years with our parents/caretakers and we have lived life the way they have shown us. Whether it was good or bad, we learned. Now we get to decide for ourselves what we think and feel. But we generally don't tend to do this, and the reason for that is that we are far too busy making ends meet and trying to get along with the society we live in. Up to this point, we constitute a by-product of our upbringing.

So, for most of us to change the effects of our upbringing, we need to take full responsibility for ourselves; this is called reaching adulthood. We then create a life that suits the person we know we are, rather than who we have been told we are. This is great, and we are free to enjoy every moment of this new life we have discovered. Then, as we move along in our journey, we start to discover that a lot of the things that our parents did we are now doing too. How is this so? The reason that this happens is that those are the traits that you chose your parents for. You want to keep them, as they feel right for you. (Remember that you are living the movie that you wrote.)

So at this point, you are still partly a result of your upbringing. Then, when you start to see the bigger picture and discover more of your truth, you reach a place where you will not know whether it originally came from your parents or not. But now it truly belongs to the you that you know yourself to be. And this is the way you will bring your children up. So in truth we are always living our own unique life and we are also living our life because of our upbringing.

Chapter 92
Essence

Your true essence cannot be affected or influenced by anything at all. Only the physical, human aspect of you gets to experience such things as pain and suffering, making love, riding a bike. There is nothing, not even death, that your essence can experience. What this is telling us is that the physical, mental, emotional, sensory human being is capable of doing things that your essence is not capable of. The old saying that you can do what you want to me, but you cannot break my spirit, is so very true. You only exist because you are an essence. The reason that the essence does not feel what you do as a human is down to your senses, which are only real in the space your body is in. They are an illusion to your essence, just as your life is.

So we find ourselves in a body that has senses that can feel, touch, taste, hear and see things. We believe that what we sense is real. How magnificent is this creation? It has to be the ultimate creation, and it is.

When you discover your essence, you understand that everything you feel as a human being is very real to that aspect of your essence. But it becomes unreal when you discover your truth. As long as you are in an Earthly body you will be in the realm of cause and effect, and time, space and separation. This is what allows us to be a separate living, thinking, talking, feeling and seeing human being. Built into all of us is the secret truth. Whether we want to acknowledge it or not at this moment, we all will eventually.

You are here on this planet, in this body, to experience things that are not possible any other way, so it is a great privilege and an honour to be involved in this thing called life. Our first role on Earth is to learn how to be a human being (as I have already said many times throughout this book). To do this right, we have to believe that is what we are. We manage this just fine. Once we have done this, then we can move on to the next stage of discovery, which is where we discover that we are more than this human being. Just as it took time and learning to know ourselves as human, it takes time and effort to know ourselves as a soul, then to know ourselves as an essence, and then to discover our self as no self, as nothing. This nothing is non-definable, and has the full potential of everything and nothing all in the moment of now, which is infinite. Remember that thought is creation but thought came from nothing, nothing being all that is and all that is not. So the potential for anything is always there, and it is thought that brings it forth and creates on every level.

Chapter 93

Recognition

We all have a need to be recognized - to be seen, heard or acknowledged in some way or other. We have a great need for other people to see who we are and what we are capable of. If you feel that the people in your life - your partner, your boss or your friends - are not recognizing you, then you will not feel appreciated for the things that you do, and you will be resentful towards those people. This does not achieve anything, so what is it that you can do to change the situation? Well, what they are not recognizing is your essence, and the reason they don't see it is because you don't shine, and this is because you have either not found your essence, or you are hiding it behind life's dramas. When you are fully present in your life there is no need for recognition. It is very nice but not essential. You know who you are and that is the most important thing to you.

So what we are really wanting when we feel that we are not recognized is for other people to say that they can see us even though we can't see ourselves. We are simply not reaching our full potential. When we require recognition for the things that we do, this is because we see ourselves in those roles - mother, lover, brother, employee, or boss. Whatever role or job we do is our choice, so why do we need someone to say how great we are at it? Is it to be of value to the world or to have a reason to be, to convince ourselves that we are needed, or to be rewarded for our hard work? We will always find a reason. What we truly need is to value our self. This is all about self-worth.

Sadly, on a physical level, we are all dispensable, and that is why we die. If we were not dispensable, then the whole human experience would not happen. The person who is here having a life is you, so why not recognize that it is you who needs to recognize yourself? Once you have achieved this, the people in your life will recognize you. If they don't it is their loss, not yours.

When other people in your life are so caught up in their dramas that they don't notice you, then in truth they are not seeing themselves. You could help them to find their truth or move on. It is up to you.

I had a hard time with recognition. I wanted the world to accept that strange phenomena did exist and that they were real. All I needed was proof. Whenever I tried to prove to anyone what I could do, it would not happen. It was as if this truth was not there to be shared. I used to get very frustrated, and then I would say to myself, it's not worth it, I am not going to doing this any more. A few days would pass and I would experience a major coincidence, or a person would phone me and tell me of their experience, and this would get me right back on track. It took me time to let go of my need for recognition, but it was what I needed to do. Then magic started to happen. I had no need to prove anything any more and, hey presto, the cause and effect interaction with the people around me started to happen. My confidence in myself grew and I just got on with doing what I do. Sometimes, when I meet someone new, I still feel that they want proof of what I am saying. I catch myself just in time, before I start justifying my work and myself.

Chapter 94
Justification

To justify is to prove to be right or reasonable. Justification is showing a reason for an action. Do we have to justify who and what we are? As far as the law of the land is concerned, we all are accountable for our actions unless we have a mental illness. It is man who has set laws on how we have to behave. If we misbehave, then we have the right to defend ourselves and justify our actions. By justifying, we are standing up for our right to be who we believe we are. As you start to discover your truth, you will feel less need to fight for your right to be. This is because you will be living and not just saying who and what you are. No one can make you think in a certain way. It is you and you alone who is in control of your thoughts. There are times when another person can use force to get you to do something, but they can never control your thoughts. It is your thoughts that tell you who and what you are.

Do I have to justify what I am writing? And could I if I had to? The answer to these questions is that I am free to think and to write whatever I want to, and you are free to read and think whatever you want to. It would only be required for me to justify my writing if I was to change your mind/thoughts. But this is not possible, for you are as free within your mind as I am. I think that having to stand up for who and what we are can cause us more harm than good. But we have laws to serve us that may, in fact, restrict us insofar as we have to define and defend our right to be.

I am not on this planet, living this life, for other people or for a particular country or race. I am here to discover my truth and live a life in order to do this. By living my truth, I will also be assisting other people to discover their truth, even if it is the total opposite of my own. The important thing here is that I am living my own truth, and I have no need to justify something that is true to me.

I have known many occasions when people have asked me to prove what I am telling them or what I believe or know. This is impossible because it is what I know, and this knowing is within my thoughts, not theirs. Just as they cannot prove their thoughts to me, even if they have a scientific explanation for them - there will always be a part missing, and that part is truth. This is not explainable. Truth is only ever knowable, but to explain knowing is impossible. And so I wonder why I am writing this book. I had to think hard to answer this question because I was trying to justify what I am doing. So here is my justification, not that I truly need one!

If by now I have convinced you to look a little deeper into your life, then you will have the opportunity to reach your truth. Not that my words alone could convince you. It would have to be that you have a connection to these words. All I can do is tell you of moments in my life and their cause and effect. The rest is up to you. I am writing this book because I can. We all live on and share this planet and we will always need laws and rules to live by, but we truly don't have to justify being here.

Chapter 95
Being

There are so many different layers that make the human form. Each layer has its own requirements. The requirements lie within the fields of science, evolution and belief. It is belief that is the most important to our existence. It is belief that allows us to exist, because we believe that we are human beings, and this is what makes it so. Belief is what allows us our place in the scheme of things. I have a belief in my physical, mental, emotional and spiritual existence, and they are all wrapped up within the form of my body. Without any one of these layers, I would not be a human being and I would cease to exist.

You may tell me that you are an atheist but that, too, is a belief. You are putting more of your belief into one layer and ignoring the layers that are truly you. You are limiting yourself to the belief that all you are is an evolved set of cells that will disappear. This is true, but you leave out the part that allows those cells to exist and to function. You might think that the brain is responsible for that. But no, the brain is the computer, and someone has to programme it. You know that the mind is programmed through experiences, but none of this is possible without the spark or the energy.

So, for anything to exist, there are many layers that work together to make it happen. As I said, without any of these layers I would cease to exist, which is death. But there is one layer that cannot cease to exist and that is energy. It simply continues to become whatever it requires itself to be. It can also continue to be without being anything at all. The energy that we use in our everyday life has always been there. We, as humans, just discover ways to use it.

The energy that is all of us, all that is, is always present. Even when this energy is used in some new way, it is only a mere fraction of that which is used for the whole planet and all who inhabit it. This life force that is energy (I am not talking Earthly energy) will know itself as a self as long as that is where it finds its self to be. If this energy were to find itself in a see-through ball, then this is what it would know itself to be. Only when that ball burst would it know it was not the see-through ball.

Whether we are talking about our mind, body or soul, we need to believe that they exist for them to be there. I believe that I am a separate human being, therefore I am. When we discover our essence, which we do not have to believe in to discover, we find that it does not believe it is our essence, for it does not know itself as a separate identity. It is pure potential. This essence is not mine or yours; it is not anyone's or anything's. It just is. Your essence is the same as my essence; so is the plant, the tree, the book, the pen, the dog. The essence is all-knowing, for there is nothing that can ever exist. That is it. But for anything to exist, it is always made up of many layers to form an idea that there is separation.

Let's take a look under a microscope at this body we have. There are trillions of cells running around, and maybe they believe themselves to be separate, doing their own thing. If you were to look at the same cells under a better microscope, then you would see that there is a substance that they are all moving within and that each one is not one but part of the whole, and that whole happens to be you. Now, if we imagine ourselves as one of those cells, and we were viewed under a microscope from somewhere in space, we would all appear to be connected within a sea of energy.

So, being a human being is an interaction of many different layers, creating the format of an individual, separate identity, which is living in a place with six billion other beings and countless different forms of substance, interacting as if they are individual when, in truth, there is one thing being trillions of things.

Chapter 96
Dimensions

There are lots of different dimensions to existence, and each of these has its own unique set of values, just as Earth has its own set of mathematical values. As the human body is made up of layers, each with its own requirements, so is what we call the universe or existence.

When you have started the journey to your truth, you reach one of these levels or dimensions with its own unique set of values, and you have to learn these in order for you to understand and know the truth within them. Remember that this learning is knowing, which is more like understanding and remembering than learning.

When a person has an experience, it is within one of these dimensions. But please remember it is easy to be mistaken into believing that any one of these dimensions is your essence, when it is not. It is just another way of being with different laws of reality. Essence is all of it, but it is not found in a dimension. It's the pure energy that makes that dimension appear to be what it is. Just as your essence is in all of you, but is not in one place. It is what allows you to exist.

There have been many occasions over the last six years when I could not believe that there could be any more to existence. And wham! bam! There before me appears something new to discover. This is not the same kind of discovery as that experienced by our normal human awareness. It is presented in a way that has to be converted into an understanding. But when it appears, I understand it. This is not in a logical, thinking way. I describe it as more of a knowing. This knowing seems to be part of my make-up. Not my physical make-up, but a level of awareness that is around and within me. It is my soul that knows what my essence is and is not.

I am sorry that I keep saying is and is not, but that is the closest I can get to describing what essence is (or is not). For there is nothing that it is and nothing that it is not (and I do know that I keep repeating this). Also, it is not something new to my soul; it is only new to my humanness. How I convert this information is impossible to describe, because we are not aware of this process. The only thing that comes close, and it's not that close, is an interpreter converting one language into another. This is very easy for some people to do and not for others, and I am among the latter. So the way I convert is very natural to me, but it would be hard for me to teach because I, as yet, don't know how I do it.

Each dimension has its own set of values and we unravel them and then move on to the next. But please don't think that we will reach the end, for there is no end - existence is infinite.

So why do we bother? Because we can, because we want to. Because this is why we exist; to discover what existing is. In order for us to discover the truth behind existence, we have to go through it and come out the other side to non-existence. Then we have to learn all about non-existence, in order to go through that and come out the other side to nothing. And when we are within nothing, we have discovered our truth, which is nothing. Here's the tricky bit: remember that this nothing is everything.

Chapter 97
Defence

We all defend our right to be, but this defence mechanism is a barrier to our truth. This defence is there to protect us in moment of attack, but I have noticed so many people wear their defence as a form of armour, as if they are called to do battle, which they are. They are protecting what is theirs and woe betide anyone who goes near them.

Scary stuff, but you must have come across it in your daily life, or maybe you do this yourself. What these people are defending is not their property or their families or even their country; they are defending their emotions, the very things that they don't like about themselves. Yes, they are protecting their frustrations, fears, weaknesses and anger.

These people are afraid that they will disappear, for their identity is so weak. It is not who they truly are. Once you are aware of the bigger picture, you don't need to defend yourself, because you don't have any great need to prove yourself, for you know who you are. That is what you are here to do, to live your life, not a false life that needs protecting. You are certainly not here to live life the way someone else wants you to. So, drop those defences and live your truth, and if you don't know what that is, then seek and you shall find.

Yes, it is fear that causes most of the problems in life. And that fear comes from not letting go and allowing life to unfold, and yourself along with it. It is all about embracing life, not encasing life.

Chapter 98
The reason

The process of life, death and beyond is what I have been talking about all the way through this book. You might now ask yourself why, and what are we here for. Well, let me now recap and attempt to summarize everything that we have covered. I will start at the beginning of the process of you; the person that you now know yourself to be. You are the result of a thought that is born to a set of parents, whether they are with you or not. This thought is as much theirs as it is yours, or you would not be here. They are there to be your first teachers. Your essence enters a new state of being and this is within the Earth dimension. Therefore, this new state of being is a separate identity - the human body. So the first thing you have to learn is how to be this being, and you must remember that the teachers you get to teach you only know what they have been taught themselves or what they themselves have experienced. The teachers help you to become that independent being you are designed to be. Whether or not they do a good job, you are going to reach a stage in life when you will start to make your own decisions about everything. Sometimes we discover that our teachers were wrong and sometimes they were very right for our way of thinking. Remember that you will think in a similar way to your teachers, as it is only with interaction with different people that you will discover new and different ways of being.

So now you can fully function within this body using its five senses. Emotions are harder to work with for they get the better of you on occasion. You are now an adult (this is not categorized by age), when you start to take responsibility for yourself. Once you have reached adulthood, you can start to mature into the being you are. But to truly do this you need to discover what makes you tick, and this applies to all levels of your being; mentally, physically, emotionally and, most important of all, spiritually.

During this process you may find there is more to you than your life teachers taught you. Most of this is in the field of belief, which no one can teach you. It is there for you to discover for yourself. They can tell you that they believe there is more to life than we think there is; the rest is up to you.

The next stage of your being a complete human being is self-realization. This happens because you discover that there is a part of you that appears to be observing you from a distance outside of your body. You may start to see life-forming patterns and everything falling into place. Life seems to make sense to you, even if you cannot explain it to others. So you go deeper into your discoveries until you reach other kinds of levels that make more and more sense to you. Then one day, out of the blue, you have an experience that blows you away. It is way beyond anything that it is possible to experience in so-called normal reality. The reason you feel this is because you were never taught that such things could happen, and the only way that you would ever believe something like this is if it happened to you. So it happens to you and this changes everything that you knew before.

This new awareness makes life all so pure and simple. Now you have had this experience. What are you going to do about it? Boy! You want to tell the world how easy it all is and what a magnificent thing this life is. So you do, and most people think that you have lost the plot. This is because they have no idea what you are talking about, and they think you don't know either. So you try to find people who have experienced something similar. And when you do, you have the most amazing connection with these people. But you know that more people should know this for themselves, so you try to discover what it was that enabled you to discover this amazing thing, and the more you look the more you find. You just keep growing and growing.

At this stage of your journey people start to notice that you seem to be happy and find life easy, and they want to know what the secret to this is. So you start to teach them what you did or did not do, and this starts them on their journey of discovery to their self. And because you assist someone on his or her journey, it also has an effect on you. You discover that the more people you help, the more you grow. The more you do, the more you know. And all of this knowing you have discovered leads you to the purpose of existence.

The purpose of being here on Earth is to know ourselves as the ultimate reality, which is to be able to create individual life, which we do very well. We acknowledge what an incredible event this is and study how it happens. This is what we do through science, which leads us to evolution. This we find amazing too, but we realize that there has to be more, to make all this happen in the first place. This is where religion comes in, our need for a belief system, a faith. This worked well for the majority of people for a long period of time. Only it is not something that we can experience personally; we are simply told how to behave in order to be part of this group. It is not that religion is wrong or right, but it is up to the individual to discover the secret truth for him or herself.

This is what has happened. Individuals started to break away from the normal way of life, because they had experienced things that were not part of any understanding they had been taught. And this led them to discover their true nature.

So why are we here on this Earth as human beings?

It is the only way to discover the truth.

The reason this is so is because the ultimate reality we find ourselves in is the furthest point away from the truth. By being a human, you are able to discover the truth, which is the ultimate non-reality, space, less than nothingness. So the only way to truly discover the truth is to be the complete opposite of that truth. (Please read this passage again.)

This means that the only way to know it (it being non-existence) is to not be it (being existence), and the only way for that to happen is to know you as a self. Not only that, but to be able to create another self, knowing itself as a self. This is the ultimate reality. So whichever way you look at it, neither can be truly known without the other, and this is also why we are on an opposite-polarity planet, to understand that one thing only exists because of the other. You can only discover what the truth is if you can discover the non-truth. We go through all of life to discover that the truth is that we are not even a 'we'. Yes, this is it, but without this journey, contained within this body, believing our self to be a separate identity, we would never be able to discover the truth. For we would never be able to look outside of our self, this self being nothing (before essence), for there is nothing there.

So putting an existence in place that can allow a fraction of the truth to live and be hidden from the truth (itself, which, in fact, is not a self) will allow us a glimpse of what the truth is.

Right, so now I have told you the secret, which is the answer to the question of life, you should be dancing, singing or standing on your head as I was.

But you will not be happy, dancing and singing, because you have not discovered what this truly means. You will not be able to, until you do it for yourself. And this is another reason that you are here, to experience and discover and truly know for yourself. We are designed as a self-contained unit with everything that is and can be inside of us. We are complete mini-universes. And the most important thing that we are is a being that has an ability to inquire and a thirst for meaning, which leads us to discover 'all that is'.

I truly hope that these words can assist you in your discovery of your truth, and that you may reach the levels of awareness that I have uncovered within myself, and experience all the pleasure that goes with it. And why am I still here on this planet? Because I continue to discover new knowing all the time, which can assist others and myself on our way.

It does not matter who you think you are - rich, poor, black, white, male, female, intelligent, stupid, good or bad - for you can never be one thing without the other. You are pure potential. We are all one in truth. If you decide that something in life has to be a certain way for you to accept it, then you are missing the point. You need to open yourself up to yourself and life to see and know the perfection in all. This is what being free is. It is freedom that ultimately allows you to discover the truth.

It is fear that causes most of the problems in life. And that fear comes from not letting go and allowing life to unfold, and ourselves along with it.

It is about embracing life, not encasing life.

Chapter 99

It is now May 2003 and what I have experienced and know now is so much more, or should I say more refined, than what I knew when I began this book. However, the most important thing that I wanted to get across then, and indeed now, is that life is a journey and a learning process within which we grow. It is something that we will all go through, so I wanted to show you this process as it unfolded.

Book Two is well under way, but I still cannot tell what it is leading to, although my typing is improving! Everything I have written about I have presented in a simple way. There is a reason for this. If I were to tell you how much I personally struggled with all the aspects and layers of my journey, and what I had to go through to get where I am now, you would not want to bother trying. You would think to yourself that you would rather live with the illusion of you than go through all of that. And I would not blame you for thinking that way. I omitted details of my suffering because it was personal to me, and mine to learn from. I learnt the hard way so you don't have to. I had to withstand and know it, all in order to fulfil my role as a teacher.

You will certainly suffer on your journey; but know that it is because you want to. When you accept this as fact, you are more than halfway there. By doing this one thing, taking responsibility for yourself and your actions, you will eliminate the need for lots of the lessons I had to endure. I was aware all along that I needed to experience these lessons in order to become a good teacher and save other people a lot of pain and confusion, not to mention a lot of time.

I have left this information to the end on purpose. It will help you if you are stuck, and it has not interfered with my teaching throughout the book. Life is what we choose it to be. Yes, it is that simple. So what you think is the first event in your life, and the rest is how you turn those thoughts into action. Everything I have written in this book is as close to the truth as I can get, and please remember that it is true because this is my life and the world, life, universe and beyond that I think it is. Therefore it is so.

That is how free we are. It is all up to you and your thoughts of it all. All you need is Love, da ta dada ta daaa ...

Lightning Source UK Ltd.
Milton Keynes UK

171200UK00001B/30/P